*...my father,
my father...*

… *my father,*
my father…

Bernard Marin
with Ian Coller

**HARVARD
PUBLICATIONS**

Harvard Publications
432 St Kilda Road,
Melbourne 3004

First published in Australia and New Zealand
by Scribe Publications, 2002
Revised reprint, Harvard Publications, 2020

Copyright © Bernard Marin 2020

All rights reserved. Without limiting the
rights under copyright reserved above, no
part of this publication may be reproduced,
stored in or introduced into a retrieval system,
or transmitted, in any form or by any means
(electronic, mechanical, photocopying,
recording or otherwise) without the prior
written permission of both the copyright
owner and the above publisher of this book.

 A catalogue record for this book is available from the National Library of Australia

The moral right of the author has been asserted.

ISBN 978 0 6485553 2 2

www.bernardmarin.com.au

Design by Skeleton Gamblers Creative

*For my wife, Wendy;
daughters, Amy and Rachel;
daughter-in-law, Deb, and son-in-law Joel;
granddaughter, Goldie, and grandson, Ziggy*

Contents

Author's Note ix
Acknowledgements xi

Prologue

The Storm 3

Part One

Jonah 9
The Patch 13
The Daredevils' Club 23
The Willow 33
Laws and Journeys 45
The Letter 59
Max 65
Home 71
Noah 79

Part Two

Winter 87
Spring 99
The River 111
Joining Up 121
Rudi 129
Mila 16 149

Part Three

The Bridge	161
The Betting Shop	167
The Dead	173
Ruth	189
Nellie	193
Brothers	199
The Last Act	213

Author's Note

My father, Private Stan Marin, was a digger. He served for almost four years as a stretcher-bearer with the 2/3rd field ambulance unit attached to the 24th Brigade in the 9th Division of the Australian and New Zealand Army Corps (Medical Corps) in Palestine, New Guinea, and Borneo.

My father was born into a Jewish family in Warsaw in 1920. The youngest of three children, he came to Australia from Poland in 1937 and enlisted in 1942. After his arrival in Australia he never saw any of his family again.

During my life with him I cannot say that I knew him. This book is my journey to understand who he was and to discover my ancestors.

I have tried in this book to preserve as much of the truth as possible. Much of the story of my father's life died with him, or with other family members, and I have endeavoured to find the best evidence available in order to fill these gaps. In the interests of telling the story truthfully, some names have been changed.

Acknowledgements

In researching and writing this book I am fortunate to have had the support of many people.

Many family members and friends, many of whom are named in the book, gave generously of their time and their memories in order to help me rediscover the past. I am truly grateful to my wife Wendy, who showed great forbearance during my journey. I thank my mother for the information she provided me in writing the book. Paul Valent's patience and insight helped me to identify the issues at stake, and to find some direction amid the confusion. During the research one of Dad's old army buddies, Rudi Jaeger, was kind enough to write me long letters which provided an irreplaceable insight into my father's wartime experiences, years which would otherwise have been lost forever. Nellie Goldberg, my father's cousin, gave me a window into the lost world of Jewish Warsaw. I mourn her passing, which sadly occurred before the publication of this book.

I am grateful for the assistance of a number of editors, researchers, and collaborators. I want to thank Jenny Lord for tireless research, Rosemary Miranda for her endless hours typing and retyping my research materials, and Brendan Cohen for helping me arrange my thoughts in the preliminary drafts.

Krystyna Duszniak provided enormous editorial and research assistance for the book, and the project may not have been possible without her help.

Lastly, it was my collaboration with Ian Coller on the manuscript which finally turned my vision into a reality. I want to thank him for bringing the eye of a writer to my story, and helping me bring my story to life.

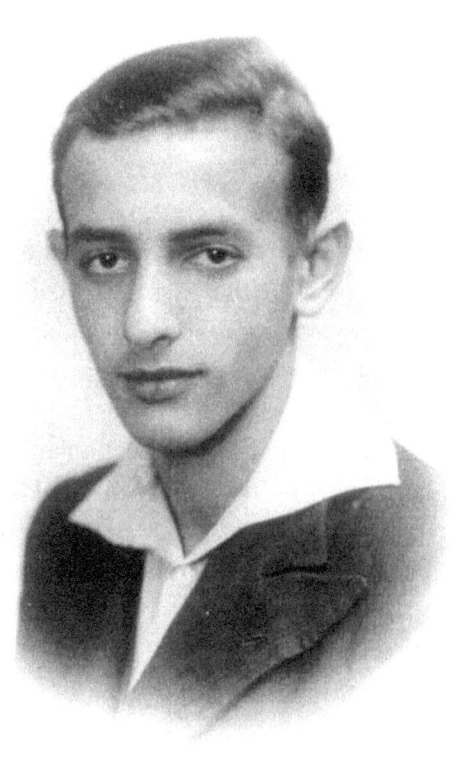

Stan Marin c.1936, just before he left for Australia

Prologue

The Storm

On holiday in Broome in 1998 I began to suffer from severe and constant headaches. What was planned as an escape from the city, a chance for us to watch the sun setting over the Indian Ocean, turned into a storm of pain inside my head. At first, I blamed the medication I hadw been prescribed for hypertension. I cut out the pills, but the pain continued unabated. At last, I resigned myself to waiting patiently for the storm to subside.

But, as the days drifted on, it only gathered in strength. Hot flushes and a racing heartbeat were followed by a dull, grey lethargy and a feeling of gasping for air. My vision was blurred as though the world had receded slightly, and I was beset by indigestion and nausea. The pain ran in jagged bolts down the right side of my face, making me dizzy and unsteady on my feet. My right eye ached as though the lid was made of sandpaper.

There were moments during this time when I wondered if I could emerge from this tempest unscathed. Constant pain has a way of wearing down one's resistance: after many days, the pain had begun to describe the limits of my world, shutting everything out. My wife and children watched, worried, and tried to help, but there was nothing they could do. They were very far away through the fog, like everything else.

At other moments, the pain seemed to bring me back to myself, as though something was waiting just over the horizon, obscured by the storm.

On my return to Melbourne I hoped the headaches would vanish like a bad dream, dispelled by the comforting familiarity of home and work among the shady streets where I'd lived all my life. But the pain was not to be so easily eluded; it returned again and again like an insistent ghost. Many times I would be forced to flee the office for hours at a time, sitting absently on the beach at Elwood, taking great panicky gulps of fresh air into my lungs while on the sands the children dug castles and moats with brightly coloured spades and buckets.

And then, all at once, I was reborn. A good friend, a doctor, found me a new migraine medication, a magic little pill. Within hours, the storm that had raged in my head had spent itself. I collapsed into a sleep which felt like a long journey: twenty, thirty hours of unconsciousness. I awoke in a house that was mine once more, and the clouded look finally began to leave the faces of my wife and my daughters.

And that, I told myself, was the end of it all. The ground beneath my feet felt stable once more, and the corners of my desk stood firm like a solid refuge. I should have been overjoyed, calm, happy. But that strange sense of foreboding, of something just beyond my gaze, had not left me along with the headache which had heralded its arrival. Much as I tried to have it otherwise, a chapter had not closed, but was only beginning.

I began to cling more and more to the medication as a way of staving off the dreaded return of this great and unwelcome disturbance in my life. One morning I looked at that small rectangular box, and I wondered how those unassuming pink tablets had come to carry so much importance for me, as though they plugged some tiny breach in myself which threatened to become a great deluge. I knew from past experience that I couldn't rely on them forever—and already the look of concern had returned to my wife's face. I had to do something more permanent. At that moment I made a decision that set me upon a journey I had to make, one which I had stalled for so long. At the time I had no idea where it would lead.

It led me to my father.

Pinkus Marin in the 1920s

Part One

Jonah

In January 1979, my father underwent a triple bypass operation. It saved his life, but only at a price: during the operation he suffered a further heart attack and stroke which left him partly paralysed, unable to work again. Not long after the surgery, I went to visit him in the hospital. I had not seen him for some time. His body lay on the white bed, barely alive, like the body of a drowned man who had been pulled too late from the wreck. It looked small and frail, surrounded by tall banks of machinery with blinking lights. It seemed to have shrunk over the years.

I stood a little way from the edge of the bed for a long time—it might have been an hour or only a few minutes. Standing in this room alone, without my family or my friends around to distract attention, I became aware for the first time of the strangeness which had opened up like a desert between us. As I watched his chest rising and falling with weak, shaky breaths, I found myself concentrating very hard, with an effort, to recognise this pale creature, this Jonah spewed forth from the belly of the fish, as my father.

I tried very hard to bring back some memory of this man. I searched for a long time, and all I could find was one evening long before when I was a very small child. My father had come into my room to check that I was asleep. I was dimly aware of his presence in the room, but I did not show that I was awake. The light was falling through the partly opened door behind his shoulder, sending warm yellow waves into my room. He stood there for a long time. Then I opened my eyes a tiny crack, and everything was dark again. He had left the room as silently as he had come. That absence, that moment before the darkness, was the only memory I could find in my heart.

It seemed to me for a time, standing there in the hospital room, that some unaccountable theft had taken place, that somehow my father had been stolen from me. And here lying before me was the warm, breathing body of the thief who had stolen my father. In his place, the thief had left a stranger: blank, distant, unreachable. And I felt a faint, dull stirring, for the first time in many years. For a moment I felt like a child again, and I felt anger at this disappearance. And I wondered if something would rise up from below, some strong feeling to save me from this strange discomfort. But nothing came. I was myself again, standing in the middle of the cold, white room.

The nurse came in, and saw me standing there in the middle of the floor.

'It's all right,' she said. 'You can hold his hand if you like.'

I looked at her, and I could see that it was expected of me. I was supposed to be the son. I waited until she had gone, then prepared myself for this strange act. As I reached out, I fought against the stark discomfort which stuck in my throat. At last, after a long hesitation, my fingers touched his hand. His skin was white and papery, with only the faintest hint of some clammy warmth, the life which held on distantly somewhere in the weakened organism. The last time I could remember his touch was as a little child, having ointment rubbed on my skin for some routine childhood malady. Between my hand and his, there was more than forty years of distance and failed affection. I wondered for a moment if now, as he lay there beached and helpless on the white bed, the time and the distance might vanish like a single breath. But it was too far and too late. I sat down, holding his hand.

I looked around the room to see if anyone was watching. I felt awkward and embarrassed sitting in the chair with this stranger's hand in mine. I moved restlessly around in the chair. I could not rid myself of the sense that I was not myself but someone else, standing in a far corner of the room, watching this farcical scene unfolding. I listened to his breaths, rasping slightly in the quiet of the room. I felt pity, sitting there watching a man's life fading away into the night. But it was the pity of a stranger. When I felt that enough time had passed, I took my hand from his, and laid his arm carefully back on the white sheet. Then I sat for a long time and stared at the patterns on the floor.

After a while I looked up and saw that my mother had come back into the room. She was busying herself with small, unnecessary duties, adjusting a bunch of anaemic-looking carnations in a yellow vase next to the window, smoothing down invisible wrinkles in the immaculate sheets on the other side of the bed. I felt an urge to ask her something about this broken, exhausted shell that lay there between us. After some time I said, 'Mum …'

She looked up from her busy, bird-like fluttering.

'I'll do what I can for him,' I said. She nodded.

I sat there for a while, wondering what I was doing there. For a moment I felt as though I was just a visitor, not a son. After a little while, I got up.

'I have to go now,' I said.

'Yes, yes,' she answered. 'We'll be fine, don't worry.' She gave me a little kiss on the cheek. Her face looked tired. I had a strange sense that, under all the appearance of anxious solicitude and motherly concern, she was actually relieved to see me go.

On the way out, I spoke to the doctor: a calm, still woman who looked at me with a certain quiet compassion. Her words were measured with the care of someone who has spoken very often to the dying. I asked her how my father was faring, and she told me that with luck he would recover within a few weeks. But, she added, the stroke had been quite severe, and we should not expect him to regain the full use of his limbs or his speech. I wondered what that meant for someone who hardly chose to speak at all anyway. From now on there would be a quite valid excuse for the yawning silences. And I can't say there was not a part of me that felt relieved of this responsibility, too. I now had a very respectable reason not to venture into the dark and uncharted waters that his growing silence left in its wake.

'He'll need some help, now,' the doctor added.

'Yes,' I said. 'Luckily, he's got Mum for all that.'

She looked at me for a moment then nodded gravely, as though she understood. I left quickly through the sliding doors, inhaling a big gulp of the cool twilight evening outside. I sat in the car for a long time before driving home. I don't remember what I was thinking about.

Six years later, in 1985, my father died. But that brief, sharp memory in the hospital room in 1979 was the last time I really thought about him for almost twenty years. And then the headaches began.

The Patch

'But the headaches are gone for good, now,' I say to my neighbour. It's 1998, a few weeks after my return from the holiday in Broome, and we are standing on the nature-strip at the front of the house. 'It's all sorted out. The wonders of medical science. Now it's time to get this garden into shape.'

'I thought something must be going on,' he says. 'I've never seen the garden anything but immaculate.'

'Yes,' I say. 'It messed up my routine.'

I look at the garden, littered with a windfall of sticks and leaves, so unlike its usual manicured orderliness. I have determined that it is time to emerge from the dimly lit rooms where I have sheltered for the past few weeks, and to devote a whole Sunday to working in the blazing light of the garden. Today is the first day I really feel confident that I am clear of the headaches at last. From time to time I still have that strange feeling, like wings fluttering behind my eyes, and the first stab of pain throbs at my temples. But I only have to swallow a couple of magic pills, and the ache melts away.

'Well,' my neighbour says, 'I'll leave you to it.'

Lately I have even begun to doubt the ferocity of the headaches—probably I really have exaggerated it. It was no more than stress and overwork, most likely. The garden is important to me. I want it to be as it was—carefully ordered and calm, a reflection of the way life should be. As it is now, it seems to cast an unfavourable light upon my state of mind. I am determined to resolve the situation quickly and painlessly. I have little patience with such complications. I start in one corner and move methodically through, pruning and trimming, weeding and sweeping. Within a couple of hours, I feel that the situation is back under control; standing upright, I feel the comforting ache in my back, and wipe the moisture from my brow. I start on the back yard.

After a while, Wendy comes out into the courtyard at the back of the house, and watches me for a little while.

I stop what I'm doing and look up. The glitter of the sun catches one of the upstairs windows with a jagged golden flash which hurts my head. Wendy is holding a white box in her hand.

'Don't overdo it,' she says. 'You're only just getting better.'

'No, really, I'm fine,' I say. 'One hundred per cent.'

'I'll send the girls out to help you,' she says.

I look at the box she is holding. For a moment I'm sure it is my box of pills.

'Can you do something about this?' she asks.

I am annoyed by this reminder of the troubles of the last months, disrupting my feeling of order and balance.

'Really,' I say, brusquely. 'I'm right in the middle of this. Can you let me finish, please?'

'It's Amy's necklace,' she says. 'The clasp is broken.'

I push the shovel down into the soil with my foot.

'I'm busy right now. I'll do it later, okay?'

I continue to weed and trim the garden beds assiduously. After a few minutes, when I glance back toward the house, she is gone.

Looking around the yard, I am disappointed by the results of my work. The garden seems even more cluttered with debris than when I began. Everything is messy and out of place. All I can see are the faults which need to be fixed.

At the back of the garden my youngest daughter Rachel has come out reluctantly to help me in my work, picking up great bundles of dead leaves and cuttings in her small arms to carry them to the compost. Small pieces of mown grass are stuck to her arms and face.

I stand up to stretch out my back, leaning back hard against my crooked arm, and I watch her from across the wide green lawn. She moves back and forth between the mounds of grass and cuttings and sticks, picking up ever-bigger armfuls in her eagerness to complete the task quickly and go back to whatever she was doing. Her brow is very faintly furrowed under the dust which has gathered from her exertions.

'You're carrying too much,' I say. 'You don't have to do it all at once.'

After a little while, predictably, she stumbles and drops an overloaded armful of rubbish she has been carrying. The path is littered with dirt and leaves, and she steps backwards, putting her foot into a flower bed. She stands for a moment, crestfallen, and bites at a nail. Then she glances across at me for a second.

'It's not a race,' I say. 'Do it properly.'

She glares at me, then kneels down and begins gathering up the fallen sticks and leaves. I watch her again. I can see the deep furrow in her small brow. The effort of her concentration jabs me with pain. I feel the sharp twinge pinching at my temple.

I feel a little dizzy. For a moment the sky is drained of colour, like a faded snapshot. From far above, I see myself standing in the middle of the garden, a strange reflection of my own need for orderliness. I watch the whole world sorting itself into beds and paths and easy arithmetical progressions. Ignoring this strange feeling, I continue momentarily along the path, cutting the regrowths of grass away from the smooth edges of the paving. Then, near the end of a row, I notice that the hot, dry summer has bitten sharply at the roots of one of the clipped English privets in the low hedge-row, its leaves turning brown from drought, its trimmed branches stiffening into brittle wooden sticks. It has spoiled the topiary effect of the border. I turn away and continue my trimming, but it bothers me, that brown stain in the careful green plan of my garden. I try to shut it out of my mind. After a few minutes, I abandon my work and dig out the dying plant. I shake the clumps of dirt off its roots, and throw the stiff brown mass onto the compost heap. But the gap that is left continues to irritate my nerves like a broken tooth. I can't settle back into the rhythm of weeding and trimming. I am annoyed at this disturbance of my schedule, and the late-afternoon sun is hurting my eyes. Looking at my watch, I wonder if I can make it to the hardware store before it closes.

'English privet?' the young man at the store says uncertainly. We are in the middle of a cavernous, impersonal warehouse stacked with endless choices of house and garden items. We walk along aisles of stepladders, banana lounges, chainsaws, cans of paint, picture frames, pergolas. He leads me towards the shrubs section, looks around, and picks up a bush randomly. 'Something like this?' he asks, half-heartedly, looking for the name on the label. 'English Box?'

'It's a border,' I say. 'The plants have to match exactly. Box and privet are two different species. You should know that.'

'If you say so,' he says.

'Is there someone here who might know something about plants?' I say, looking around.

He calls his boss, an older man with a taciturn air, who listens to my problem silently.

'Won't find it here,' he says, almost with satisfaction. 'Ran out of 'em last week.'

My disappointment is evident. I think of that disquieting gap in the hedge, and realise it's now too late to fix it this weekend. It will bother me at work during the week, in odd times during meetings and sending emails and reading sheets full of figures—the sense that something is missing, something is out of place.

'Is there anywhere else around here?' I ask. 'There's got to be another shop open somewhere.'

He thinks for hardly a moment before he shrugs.

'It's Sunday afternoon,' he says. 'We're pretty much all there is around here.'

'Forget it,' I say, stiffly. 'I'll just drive until I find something.'

As I drive, I become aware of the landscape subtly shifting and changing. In the distance, the mountains appear from the horizon. The trees change from the planes and beeches of the inner suburbs into clumps of eucalypts and tree ferns. I am driving past stretches of highway-side shopping malls and acre-lots of used cars and office-supply warehouses. Then I turn off the road and follow a path through winding streets that I hardly remember. They are now lined with houses and yards, kids playing in avenues, ovals and parks and dry creek-beds surrounded by pockets of forest. Several times I think that I am lost, but then I find again a landmark I recognise, and drive deeper into the maze of streets. Finally, I decide to give up this ridiculous and hopeless quest. I turn back towards the highway, and then I pass it, squealing on my brakes and reversing rapidly. A nursery.

I get out of the car and walk toward the green-netting-covered hurricane fence at the front of the nursery. It is closed. But on the nature-strip there is a profusion of potted plants which have not yet been taken inside. Among them is a small English privet, not terribly flourishing, but healthy nonetheless. It will certainly do, and I feel relieved at having successfully staved off the projected week's anxiety. I look through the fence, and in the last rays of the afternoon sun I can see someone, a man, moving around among the rows of plants on wooden slats. I am just about to call out when I notice a little boy, about five or six, with a watering can, walking behind the older man. He staggers from pot to pot, unsteadily pouring water onto the plants. The watering can is heavy, and it takes most of the child's strength to lift it.

I am a long way from home. I am aware of my own absurdity in driving an hour to locate a shrub. I am a little worried by my own desperation. And the fluttering wings of the headache are beginning to beat faster behind my eyes. But in the face of that little boy I can see something which has not been part of my life for many years.

For the first time in twenty years, I remember that I once had a father. Not the pale stranger lying on the bed in the hospital room, but a warm, alive man, in a dark nineteen-fifties suit, with his shirt sleeves rolled up, standing in the middle of the potted herbs and geraniums and rhododendrons of his nursery in Ferntree Gully. In the face of this child I can see the same idiotic childish pride I felt every Sunday afternoon at being allowed to assist my father with the business of planting and growing and watering and weeding. Sometimes I helped the local gardeners pick out the shrubs and rockery plants for their quarter-acre blocks and nature strips: pigface, agapanthus, Chinese lanterns, spider plants, zinneas, pink and violet fuchsias, crimson azaleas, white hibiscus. I was captivated by this profusion of life and colour, this certainty, this love.

It was an irreplaceable Australian institution, the local nursery of the nineteen-fifties, bursting with the botanical splendour of local and imported flora, from bottlebrush to bougainvilleas, from kangaroo paw to camellias, along with ranks of potting mix and rockery-features, miracle-gro and aphid spray, shovels and weedkillers. My father's nursery was called 'The Patch'. It was here on the edge of the city, in the eastern reaches of the Melbourne suburbs, where the foothills of the Dandenongs begin the steep rise toward densely forested peaks. I wonder if that is, after all, why I have come. I would like to believe that this is the same nursery, that it is still here after more than forty years. But I know that The Patch is gone long ago, hidden beneath the rolling suburbs, buried under layers of grey concrete.

And buried, too, is my thriving little vegetable garden which I tended religiously at the back of the nursery. All weekend I pottered and basked in the sense of security and closeness of being together with my father in the bright clear sunlight. Sometimes he talked nearby with friends and business acquaintances and customers. I do not remember the conversations—the low, reassuring murmur was all I needed to understand. Meanwhile, I wandered up and down the gravelled rows with a watering can, watching the seedlings poke their first green shoots above the moist earth. In the permanent noon of childhood I believed that the sun would always be shining, and the sprinklers always glistening, and that my father, that man in dark grey pants, his sleeves rolled up to his elbows, would be there, always murmuring or laughing around the next row of gardenias.

But he wasn't. Somewhere along the way he became that stranger who lay on the hospital bed, that pale shell, that Jonah. What happened? I remember the dry, empty feeling of that room, twenty years ago, a feeling I have learned to accept. But now I am taken off guard once again by the memory of some real happiness, by the memory that there was once a time when I had a father. I feel sick, confused by the memory of that child following among the branches heavy with blossom, among the small pots of violets. I can hardly bear it. I feel the headache bearing down on me with increasing force. I can't stay here any longer. I put down the plant and go back to the car. On the drive back to the city the sun is slanting directly into my eyes, a glaring mass bouncing off the asphalt of the highway. I drive faster, trying to make it home before the tidal wave of this headache breaks over me.

I walk up toward the house, alone in the darkening stillness of the garden, past the gap in the border with the hole dug ready for the privet. I regret not buying it now, and I wonder what could have come over me to drive such a long way for nothing at all. The headache is worse. How ridiculous, I think. I'll get my secretary to ring them tomorrow. Then I realise I have no idea what the name of the nursery is. I need to go inside and take a tablet. On the table under the eaves I notice a small white object—an enamelled box belonging to Amy, my older daughter. It is the box that Wendy was holding earlier, when she stood here in the courtyard. I remember thinking that it was the pills she had come to talk to me about. I'll fix it now, before I go inside, I think—I'm not so dependent on the pills that I can't wait a moment. I open the box, and inside is a necklace of amber beads which has come apart, the clasp no longer attached to the string, the beads spilling out of the box. I rethread the small beads onto the rope and attempt to secure the clasp, tying and retying the end of the string which holds the fastener. I never really learned to tie knots. I try tying it one way, then the opposite way. After a while, I test the knot I have made, and the beads spill off onto the concrete. I crawl around gathering them up to start threading them again. While I'm gathering them up, Wendy comes out into the courtyard.

'Bernard,' she says, her pale, calm face gazing down on me with a look of surprise. 'What on earth are you doing?'

I look up at her, and I am frightened by the concern in her voice, the creases which invade her smooth forehead. It is not me that is the object of this concern. I feel a thousand miles away from here.

'I can't put this back together,' I say. Her forehead is smooth, and she smiles again, her calm, slightly distant smile.

'Well, don't worry about it. It's not that important,' she says.

'No, I have to do it now,' I say. 'If it takes me all night.'

She shakes her head and shrugs.

'Well, don't stay out here too long,' she says. 'It's getting cold.'

In bed that night, I wonder what is happening to me. And in spite of the medication I can still feel the headaches beating their wings in the distance, ominously. After Wendy is asleep, I get up and take a couple more pills. I have my life, and my family, and my business. I refuse to let this chaos take control. I will drive it away, whatever it takes.

Then it all starts again a few weeks later.

The Daredevils' Club

Saturday morning. The routine is a familiar and easy one—getting up a bit later than usual, a swim at the pool, breakfast with the kids, who are excited about the weekend opening up before them, and not yet struck with the irritable lethargy which descends by Sunday afternoon. Then the short drive to the Malvern shops which I could make in my sleep, the usual parking spot behind the grocers, and the reassuring rhythm of the crowd as shoppers swarm up and down Glenferrie Road. They peer into shop windows against the glare, dragging or chasing recalcitrant youngsters, and murmuring to one another in a pleasant hum. I am happy to be held fast by this familiar, unsurprising routine. Wendy has to run up to the pharmacy. 'Wait here just a minute,' she says. 'Don't go anywhere. I'll be back.'

I wait by the fountain in the tiled plaza across from the white turret rising from the town hall, watching the faces of the people passing by. A young couple push a pram across the busy street. A group of boisterous teenagers jostle by, talking too loudly, as though pleased by the sound of their voices. An elderly man struggles past, lost in the concentration he needs to complete his morning constitutional.

Then among these faces one strikes me oddly—it's not quite familiar, but it's not the face of a stranger, either. Instead there is something, a flicker of a gesture or the way his eyes crease, which stirs a strange recognition. He is wearing a beige cap, perhaps because he is losing his hair. I catch his eye, and he looks away momentarily, then looks back. After a moment he smiles, and walks toward me. As he gets closer I rack desperately through my archive of names and situations—it's going to be embarrassing if I have to ask him his name.

'Bernard?' he says. I nod. 'Wow, it's really been a long time. It must be almost twenty years. How are your family these days?' I can see that we must have been kids together. But I still can't remember his name. I try to picture him with more hair, without his moustache, but no luck.

'Well, Mum's fine. My dad passed away years ago now,' I say. For some reason, I hope that he won't ask me any more about that.

'Yes, I did hear about that. I'm sorry. What about your brother?'

'Paul's fine. He's practising law. He's a barrister.'

'Married?'

'Yes, but he separated from with his wife recently.'

'And you—you're married, kids?'

'Yes, two. Two girls.'

'Wow,' he says. 'Can you believe it? You know, only the other day I was telling my son stories about us when we were kids. Do you remember that Daredevils' Club we used to have? God, jumping off the garage roof. I'd never let my son do it. Different time then, though. Safer. Do you remember?' He laughs.

'Not really,' I say. There's an uncomfortable silence.

'So it must be, what, ten years ago that your dad died?' he asks. I nod.

'So,' I ask, 'who was it that started up the club?'

'Oh,' he says. 'Well, it must have been Paul, and maybe a couple of the others. You and me, we were that bit younger, so we always had to be the followers. Paul was the real daredevil, of course. He was forever getting into trouble with your dad.'

'Really?' I say. 'I don't remember much about it.'

'Oh yeah,' he says. 'Your dad was a bit of a character. Bought you a couple of brand new Malvern Star bicycles, out of the blue, must've cost a fortune in those days. I was really jealous, harped on to my mum all the time about it. Then one day I was in the yard and I could hear your dad screaming "You fucking idiot, Paul!" After that I shut up about the bikes. I guess I thought maybe you weren't so lucky after all.'

'That's true, I suppose,' I say, and shrug. 'Paul fought with him a lot. I didn't.'

'He was sick, wasn't he? I remember one day—it must have been a few years later—I was at home visiting my parents. I saw him getting out of the car,' he says. 'He looked twenty years older. He was walking with a stick. It was a bit of a shock.'

'He had a stroke,' I say. Then I don't feel like talking any more. He starts to tell me about his family, but I interrupt and tell him I have to go and catch up with my wife. 'She's waiting for me,' I say.

That night, lying in bed, I can't sleep. I lie on my side, my back, but my thoughts never begin to slow into a sleepy pattern. The headache is bothering me again. I get up and go downstairs to the kitchen to take another pill. A light rain has fallen, and through the windows I can see a vague reflection of moonlight glistening into the courtyard. I can hear a tap dripping somewhere, a faint, irregular tattoo of drops. Every half-a-minute or so, just when you think it has stopped, it comes again. Rat-a-tat-tat-tat. Suddenly I notice that I have been standing in the kitchen for a long time. I'm not really sure how long, or what time it is. For some reason, now the name of the man in the beige cap is in my head: Alex Korman. It surprises me that I should have forgotten. I think about him as a child; smaller even than me, although around the same age.

And I remember the end of the fifties, when I was only nine or ten, and Paul started the Daredevils' Club. The older boys in the street had been picking on him, and he started the club as a way of distracting their attention or obtaining their respect. The idea of such a club was irresistible to the boys of the street. As numbers are required for such activities, to compel everyone to appropriate acts of idiocy and to provide an appreciative audience, even Alex and I were allowed to join.

The club began relatively harmlessly, with such heroic acts as jumping off the garage roof. It looked easy from below, but the first time I climbed up I was terrified into the pit of my stomach. I stood up there, looking across the lawn at the roof of our house, at the trees in the garden and the cars going past on the road, wondering if I would ever see any of it again. Inside, I knew, my father would be reading the sports page silently, lifting up his feet so that my mother could vacuum under them. I could imagine my mother's anxious face when she heard that I had been injured. I could see her bustling here and there, nervously, getting cross with me, never at home in a crisis. Then I thought of my father, and wondered what he would think, if he would be angry, or worried, or simply indifferent. Then, while thinking about this, I stepped out into space, and lurched forwards, tumbling toward the ground. I landed on my feet and one arm, and rolled sideways. Fortunately the thick bed of couch grass which passed as a lawn in the late 1950s provided a landing-cushion. I got up unsteadily, and was congratulated by the other boys, feeling the first small thrill of acceptance.

But Paul had climbed onto the garage roof, and then onto the roof of the house, a few feet higher up. He was calling everyone to watch. The boys milled around under the roof. I called up 'Paul, you're going to get into trouble.' Paul just shouted at me to get lost, and jumped towards the lawn. He hadn't come quite close enough to the edge of the roof before jumping, and so his leap fell just short of the lawn, his foot hitting instead a wood and canvas folding chair which was standing at the edge of the patio, with a loud crash of splintering wood. There was a shocked silence among the boys. Then Paul limped to his feet, and began to laugh, almost hysterically. The other boys crowded around him, talking excitedly. Within a minute or so the front door swung open and they scattered. My father stormed towards us. Seeing the broken chair, he walked straight past me and grabbed Paul by the arm, dragging him into the house. As they passed me I saw a strange look on Paul's face, almost a look of satisfaction.

At first we were sated by the heady thrill of jumping into space from assorted roofs, the satisfaction of conquering our fear and causing what mayhem we could. But Paul was on the look-out for more authentically perilous activities. No matter how much trouble he got into for one escapade, he was only fired with enthusiasm for something more dangerous. Finally he made up his mind that we should carry out a theft in Davies' paper-shop. The other boys were filled with excitement at doing something not simply dangerous but actively wrong. This time we would be demonstrating a thrilling contempt not for the laws of physics, but for everything we had been taught by rote every morning at school assembly. We would cheerfully disobey our parents, teachers, and the law. It would be a marker of our independence, our manhood, our outsider status. We all agreed to the plan.

But once we were outside the newsagents, our resolve weakened. The wide brown hessian doormat marked a fateful threshold to be crossed, an act whose consequences could not be foreseen.

'So who's gonna do it?' someone asked. There was a silence.

Paul looked around the boys with scornful bravado. 'I reckon we should all take something. That's fair.'

'I don't know,' I said. 'We might get in trouble.'

Paul looked at me scornfully.

'Shut up, goody-goody, you're gonna do it,' he said. 'Or else you're out of the club.'

Everyone agreed, rather reluctantly, unwilling to come off as a chicken. But just before we went in, Alex Korman remembered that he had a doctor's appointment and had to go home.

'Go on then, sissy.' Paul said.

A few of the others looked like they might have doctors' appointments, too, but Paul hustled them inside before a mass desertion could take place. For some reason, he was strangely intent on the success of this escapade. At any rate, it would put a final stamp on his leadership of the group.

But inside the shop, it was a fiasco. The boys tried to act

inconspicuous, which drew attention even more strongly to their loitering. A couple kept looking around nervously, and at least one boy looked like he was about to make a bolt for it. The whole weight of middle-class morality bore down on us, destroying any chance we had of acting coolly under such circumstances. Fortunately, the newsagent, Mr Davies, was tying up a pile of newspapers, and so failed to register this farcical comedy happening in front of him.

I moved among the racks stacked high with copies of *Sporting Globe*, *Women's Weekly*, and *Australasian Post*, past tins of picture corners and pots of glue, and locked glass display-cabinets of pipes and pens. I was trapped in an agony of guilt and fear, like a guilty shade flickering between the piles of magazines on one side, and the HB pencils and bottles of ink on the other. Then, after a while, I remembered that I was supposed to steal something. I put my hand out tentatively toward a packet of bulldog clips on the edge of a stand.

Just at that moment, one of the loiterers suddenly stirred and moved towards the door, sparking a rush from the rest of the boys. I went, too, spurred by a physical panic of nervous energy. A couple of boys got out in time, but the proprietor suddenly stood up and saw the scene unfolding before him. I froze, and was grabbed, along with Len Fein and Steven Jacobs, and we were forced to turn out our pockets. None of us had anything. The newsagent looked nonplussed. He was about to let us go, when he noticed Paul at the other end of the shop. I was relieved. Paul would no doubt have had time to put back whatever it was that he had stolen, and we would all leave scot free, with only our nerves a little jangled.

'Come over here,' Mr Davies said. Paul walked coolly over. 'Empty your pockets.' Paul stood there, defiant. 'I said, empty your pockets,' Mr Davies repeated, angrily.

Paul slowly and gracefully took everything out of his pockets. A handkerchief, a key, some coins, a marble, assorted bits of paper, and lastly a pack of playing cards still in their wrapper, with the shop's price sticker on the front.

'Nice try, sonny,' Mr Davies said. 'I'm sick to the back teeth of brats like you. I should really call the cops. Then you'd really find out what trouble is.' Paul arched an eyebrow, but he blanched slightly.

'It was only a dare,' I said. Paul looked at me blankly. Mr Davies looked us over and sized up the situation.

'Yes, well count yourself lucky if I only call up your mum and dad this time. Next time—well, there better not be a next time, if you know what I mean.'

'Yes, sir,' I said.

'And what about you?' Mr Davies asked Paul.

'Yeah. Okay.' Paul said.

When we got outside I said to Paul, 'Why didn't you dump it when he caught us? Now Dad's gonna do his nut.'

Paul said 'Oh, shut up. Who cares?' He walked off. I followed him. 'Piss off,' he said. He walked away, leaving me alone. I went to Alex Korman's house for a while, and told him all about it. I stayed there until I heard the clinking of the dinner table being laid out, and slunk home, fearing the catastrophe about to descend on my head.

By chance, Dad was not home when the newsagent telephoned. My mother took the call during dinner, and I watched her as she nodded gravely. She did not turn to look at us. She listened for quite a while, and then apologised to Mr Davies in a low voice. I flinched at her humiliation. She hung up the phone, and stood for a few moments with her back to us. Then she went into the kitchen and began washing the dishes. After a few minutes, the phone rang again, and she answered it. I heard her listening for a while, then gauged from her answers that the caller was the mother of one of the other club members. My mother didn't say much during the call, and finally she said, 'Yes, all right, Miriam. I'm not sure. I'll think about it.' She hung up the phone, and turned around to us. Her face, usually masked by the slightly wounded, solicitous look she felt appropriate to the role of a mother, was for once unusually open. For one moment she looked at us like equals who might help her make a difficult choice.

'Mrs Korman thinks I shouldn't tell your father. You know how upset he will be. She is worried he will lose his temper.'

There was a silence. We stared at her, unsure of what to say. I prayed that she would take this excellent advice. I promised in future to think more charitably about Mrs Korman's smelly dog, and her constant discussion of her lumbago. But Mum was evidently undecided. Her flickering hesitation made even more sickeningly evident the gravity of the situation. Even Mrs Korman was afraid of what might happen. I went and sat in my room, and waited for the axe to fall, the minutes ticking by interminably.

The prospect of my father's anger occupied me. I had never understood it—it would blow in from nowhere like a sudden dust-cloud, and then disappear again, just as suddenly, into the calm, grey sky. It was usually associated with some new provocation or act of defiance by Paul, but it always seemed to have some other element—a kind of passionate fury which exceeded the circumstances. It rarely resulted in actual violence, but rather in an impotent rage, which Paul seemed to derive some strange satisfaction from provoking. I had always felt excluded from this strange symbiosis, always trying instead to please my father through obedience and righteousness. This earned me the vengeance of my brother, who had taken to venting on me his powerlessness in relation to my father. And this often led to his being punished once again. Thus, somehow, we had become cast irrevocably as the bad son and the good son, the delinquent and the angel. They were parts which we played up to, and which slowly became unquestioning elements of our respective selves. Doubtless they drew upon some fundamental grain of our personalities, but they grew into a dynamic whose strength I never quite understood, even as it shaped the complexion of my childhood. Now I was sure that this bubble of virtue which had so far protected me was burst forever, that Paul and I would henceforth be seen as equally bad, and receive equal shares of my father's anger.

After a long time, I heard a noise from the front of the house, the click of the key in the lock, and the familiar sounds of my father's arrival home. I crept out of my room toward the kitchen, and heard the sound I dreaded most—my mother talking to my father in a low, serious voice. I fled back to my room, and lay paralysed on my bed for what seemed like hours. After a while—I'm not sure how long—I fell asleep. When I woke up, I was still in my clothes, lying on the bed, the house darkened and quiet. I walked around the house as though in a dream. Nothing stirred, everything was still and cold.

I went back to my bedroom and changed into my pyjamas. Before getting into bed I remember standing in the middle of the room, my bare feet cold against the floor, shivering a little, listening hard. Everything was silent. In the distance I could hear the occasional clanking of a street sweeper or, far away, a dog barking faintly. I felt completely alone, as though my family had disappeared forever into the night, leaving me behind.

I awoke the next morning to a silence which was never broken. My father was not angry with me, nor did he lecture me, or laugh. He avoided me all that day, and the next. Within a week, the matter was forgotten. When I realised I would not be punished for my part in the crime I felt a cool relief wash over me. But somewhere in my heart it felt as if a door had closed against me. I could have borne my father's anger, perhaps. But every time he avoided my eyes, I felt I had been banished, sent to some faraway place, getting smaller and smaller until I was out of sight.

Back in my own kitchen, the distant tap comes again with its rat-a-tat-tat-tat. That night of my childhood feels as close as the tips of my fingers. Was it from this moment that I date my sense of abandonment, the loss of my relationship with my father? Now, standing here as a man of almost fifty, the whole affair seems like a trivial reminiscence. After all, I had not actually committed any crime, and I was not punished for it. Yet that moment in the empty house was the first time that I felt how my father had turned away from me. And I, too, began to learn how to live on this new, strange, cold planet; how to look after myself and my own survival; how to shut myself off from the world. But now, after forty years, it doesn't seem to be working any more. I look at the box of pills in front of me, and I wonder where I am going.

Suddenly it seems miserably cold in the kitchen, and I feel tired to my very bones, as though I have walked for miles in the cold, wet night. I'm sure I look ridiculous, standing here shivering in my pyjamas. I take the pills and walk back through the stripes of moonlight on the floor. I climb the stairs to bed, and sleep a dreamless sleep.

The Willow

Later in the week Paul comes over. My brother is chronologically older than me, but these days he seems more than ten years younger. 'Chalk and cheese,' Wendy always adds whenever she has to describe us to other people. Paul stands around with self-conscious ease in the kitchen. With his tight black top and flared jeans, his long, curly hair falling to his shoulders, he leans against the cupboard, talking to Wendy. He chats casually about his practice as a barrister and the unconventional—one might say criminal—clients he defends. I notice that he enjoys playing up the sense of adventure, excitement, uncertainty of his job. He makes a point of saying that the only thing holding him here in the suburbs is his commitment to his kids.

Paul plays a game of table tennis with Rachel, and I listen to their shouts of competitive excitement coming from the other room. He seems at home in my house. I have changed out of my suit after work, but a certain stiffness, a certain formality, an air of the office, always lingers not far away. I wonder what it is that made him end up so different from me, still so energetic and unconventional, so centred on youthfulness, while I have chosen, equally deliberately, this role of father, husband, committee member, pillar of the community. When I look at the photographs of us as children I am always the one standing back slightly, diffidently, retreating a little from the camera. Paul is full of restless energy, edging forward—one always has the feeling that he is about to burst out of the frame. And he is no different now, creeping reluctantly into his fifties—he still echoes the same quest for novelty and excitement, the same impatience and distracted intelligence. To me, his life is too disorganised, chaotic. I can't see how he can stand it. When I make a gesture to help, it always seems clumsy and pompous, and he quickly becomes exasperated—a set response. Yet we manage to maintain a strong relationship nonetheless. Sometimes I wonder if it is the bond of two orphans.

After Rachel has gone to bed, Paul sits with me in the study.

'She's not too bad at table tennis,' he says. 'I need to improve my game.'

'Yes,' I say. 'I try to make sure that I teach them this stuff that Dad never taught us.'

'I don't know why you blame it on Dad,' Paul says. 'He wasn't that bad.'

'I didn't say he was bad. He just never taught us, that's all.'

'Well, I just learned things for myself. And I did pretty well, so what does it matter?'

'There are some things you never learn unless you have someone to teach you.'

'Like what?'

I don't reply. I'm not sure where I am going with this.

'Look,' Paul says, 'Dad had his problems. God knows, we fought enough. You're the one who got along with him.'

'Because I didn't fight with him?'

'Yeah. You never got into trouble with him. You were always the good son.'

'I didn't choose that. Did you choose to be the bad one?'

'Well, it was just my character. Anyway, it wasn't all fighting.'

'Really?' I say. 'What else do you remember about him, apart from the fighting?'

He stares at me. He looks as if he is about to reply.

But he doesn't say anything for a long time. He looks away.

'I know there were other things,' he says. 'I just can't think of them now.'

'Okay,' I say. 'Do you ever remember him coming to one of your football matches?'

'Yeah,' Paul says, 'I think he came a couple of times.'

'And that was it, right? He just couldn't be bothered. He never came to a single one of mine.'

'You know he was a workaholic. He just worked all the time. So maybe he didn't have the time. Why do you get so worked up about it? It's so long ago.'

'Well, I would have given anything for him to come just once. But he never did.'

Paul leans back in his chair. He looks uncomfortable, irritated by the conversation. He stares at me, then he gets up, like a spring uncoiling.

'I've got to go,' he says. 'I have someone waiting for me.'

A few weekends later, Wendy and I go to the kids' school sports. We sit on the sidelines watching Amy running against the other children, a typically odd assortment of heights and personalities. We cheer her on, and congratulate her when she comes over. She has come second in a field of eight.

'Don't worry,' I say. 'You'll definitely come first next time. Practice makes perfect. Most of the other kids don't have any discipline. If you stick at it, you'll win.'

Amy listens silently, and nods. Then she runs off to join the other kids. Wendy and I sit for a while in silence.

'Is that really what you think?' she asks.

'What do you mean?'

'Well, she came second, after all. You're very focused on winning.'

'Well, I want them to try hard, and reap the benefits. They can achieve anything they want to in life.'

'But she doesn't have to.'

'Why shouldn't she? She's just as good as the other kids. Better, in fact.'

'Well, she can find that out for herself. You don't have to push her.'

'Okay, fine,' I say. 'Next time I won't say anything.'

I sit there in silence, fuming. My head starts to throb with pain. Then I realise I haven't brought my tablets with me.

'I have to go,' I say.

'You're not sulking, are you?' Wendy says. 'It was just an observation.'

'No, I just have a headache,'

'Oh, not again.' Wendy sighs. 'Can't you stay until the end? It's only an hour or so.'

'There's nothing I can do about it,' I say, irritably. I can't think of anything except getting home to get rid of the haze of pain which is descending over everything.

'Well, you can't just keep taking those drugs all the time. Maybe you'd better see someone.'

'Don't be ridiculous,' I say. 'It's just a bloody headache.' Wendy looks taken aback.

In the car, I wonder why I am so angry about nothing. Wendy is obviously right about the race. I'm acting like a child. When I get home, I take a tablet, and then sit in the study, waiting for the drug to take effect, lying with my head back. From that angle I notice an old shoebox sitting on the very top of the bookshelf, and I stare at it. After a while I get up and climb onto the lower shelf in order to get it down, sprinkling myself with dust in the process. Inside are a collection of various sporting mementos and annuals which I have kept for almost forty years. They are the legacy of an obsession with sport which dominated the later part of my childhood. By the age of twelve I was already playing sport like a demon; at school, after school, every Saturday, all through the holidays. Cricket in summer, football in winter. I clutched my willow cricket bat at the crease and in the nets hour after hour with a desperate enthusiasm I can still almost feel. Perhaps I felt that I found an acceptance and belonging on the oval and the cricket field which I would never find at home. Perhaps I believed that if I shone brightly enough on the field—as I would never do at school—my father would be won over to some connection I still imagined possible.

At the bottom of the box are a cricket cap from the Ormond Under-16 B Premiership team of 1965, and the bails I took from the wicket at the end of that historic game. It is the legacy of the overriding passion of my childhood. I can't explain fully to an outsider the fascination of this game which exercised such a grip over my life. I watched the scratchy images on our black-and-white Admiral television set with an unbreakable concentration I never mustered for any other activity. I was lost in an endless admiration of stroke and block, offspin and googly. I idolised the god-like test players, whether Australian, English, West Indian, Pakistani: Richie Benaud, Garfield Sobers, Colin Cowdrey. I daydreamed my way through schoolwork and leisure, imagining the moment I would step out onto the green pitch of Lords, the MCG, or the WACA in the glorious battle for the Ashes. I pored over Wisden, imagining my batting scores up there among the constellations. I knew it was a long way to Lords from the Ormond Under-16s, but my imagination soared high above such details.

My father never showed up at a single game. While the other parents squabbled and elbowed their boys onto the eleven, and cheered from the sidelines with the furious, one-eyed barracking of Australians everywhere, my father always 'had to work' or 'needed to finish something'. Dad had been to a few of Paul's football games in the past, so I hoped that if I played well enough, and behaved myself at home, he might decide to come along to mine. But any limited store of fatherly feeling that Dad possessed seemed to have burnt up like a struck match-head on the tentative efforts with Paul, which had almost universally ended in disaster. Whether it was sport, mathematics, or making a go-cart, my father had little understanding of the limitations of a child. And Paul responded to Dad's impatience in his own irrepressibly wilful and defiant manner. So inevitably such interactions spun out of control, and ended in some kind of embarrassment, misunderstanding, or argument. By the time it came to me I could see that my father had already given up. Sometimes I felt as though I'd been born under an invisible curse, like the younger son in a fairy tale.

I desperately wanted my father to come to a game. Sometimes I looked across while I was batting to see if his smaller, paler face was standing out among the red stubbly faces of the cricket dads, his inevitable cigarette trailing a thin line of smoke. I had learned long ago that I wasn't allowed to ask him to come. But as every new season came and went I couldn't help imagining that things would be different. Then, at last, we won the Under-16 B premiership, and I even rated a mention in the club annual. I underlined the tiny piece of print and carried it home in my hands, looking at it repeatedly, as if to reassure myself of my own value. I felt that this tremendous achievement must surely warrant some notice, even an unimaginable congratulation from my father. And perhaps it would make him see that it was worth showing up once in a while.

I found my father in the backyard, reading his paper and smoking, as usual. He was in one of those silent motionless states which I noticed more and more often as I grew older. I pulled out the club annual and gave it to him in silence. He looked at it, nodded mutely, and gave it back.

'Maybe …' I began. 'It would be great if you could come along and see a game next season. I'm doing really well, and next year it's the under-17s. I might even be in the As.'

My father looked at me and slowly breathed out a mouthful of smoke. He looked away.

'You'll never be tall enough to be an opening batsman,' he said.

I was a bit stunned. I stood there for a moment in silence, not sure what to say.

'Well, Bradman wasn't all that tall, you know. You don't have to be … tall,' I stammered.

He shrugged and turned his newspaper over.

After a moment, he heaved himself up out of the folding chair with an effort and said irritably, 'I don't know why you try so hard. It's a waste of time.'

I flushed. He stared at me for quite a while, and shook his head.

'No matter how good you are, you're never going to play for Australia.'

He stood there for a moment. It was as if he wanted to say something more. But he just shook his head, and turned away. As he walked off, he said, over his shoulder, 'They'd never pick a Jew.'

I can still hear my father's low voice, with its heavy accent, spitting this comment out as he walked away. It sounds out in the back of my mind, over and over. I put the bails and the cap and the annuals back in the box, and hoist it back onto the top shelf. I have to drive back to the sports ground to pick up Wendy and Amy. I switch on the radio to drown out his voice, but every channel seems to jangle my nerves even further. Despite the medication, the headache is coming back with a vengeance. When I arrive at the ground, Wendy looks at my pale face and says, 'You'd better let me drive.'

Most of the drive home is silent. I feel like I should say something.

'I'll make an appointment with Goldman tomorrow.'

Wendy doesn't say anything.

The painting in the waiting room is very familiar—no wonder, really, since it was a present that I gave Dr Goldman many years ago. It is a print of a nineteenth-century beach scene by Prendergast, the pastelly water-colours representing my idea of tranquillity and escape from the complexities of ordinary life. I've had therapy a few times in the past, and I gave Dr Goldman this print after my last session, more than a decade ago, to mark the end of that part of my life. I am pleased to see that he still has the picture—it makes me feel more in control of this situation. It is strange to be looking at this picture at all. After all, I bought it as a sign that I had sorted everything out, that my life would unfold in these attractive colours, a little idyll of family happiness. And after all, I think to myself, you haven't done so badly. You are a survivor. A survivor. You have pulled yourself from the depths of despair before. You can work through this. You have a loving wife, two beautiful daughters, a nice house, a satisfying career. You're a success. Yes, you're a success.

I stand up and wander around the room. If it weren't for these headaches ... that's really the problem. Simple pleasures—that's all I want out of life. Just waking up in the mornings free from pain. You've suffered enough, I think you deserve some kind of comfort. I look at the Prendergast print again. I wonder how it is that I am back here looking at this scene and waiting for the doctor again. I look down the corridor. It feels like I am waiting for a long time, which annoys me. I can't be bothered to read a magazine. I look closely at the picture again to distract myself for a minute or so at least. The sea is painted in swirling brush-strokes of blue—a nice effect. The beach is yellow and pink, like the sands along the peninsula. The people are cleverly sketched in with a few strokes, a group of smartly dressed picnic-makers. Perhaps I should take up painting—I'm sure I could learn to paint like this if I had a few lessons. I check to see how he has painted the people, and I notice that they are just clothes and gestures—an umbrella, a blanket. They don't actually have any faces. It's quite clever, I suppose, but it irritates me a little that the painter hasn't bothered to fill in the detail.

Dr Goldman appears at the door. His consulting rooms are just as they were. It feels a little like stepping back thirteen years. But I remind myself what a success I have made of my life since then—it's completely different. Dr Goldman sits on the chair next to his roll-top desk, in the same place next to the wall. I sit opposite.

'I'm glad to see you still have that print,' I say. 'It all looks just the same.'

He nods, and waits for me to tell him what I've come to see him about.

'I'm sure it's nothing, really,' I say. 'Everything has been fine since I saw you last. I'm married now, children, career. I'm very happy.'

'Yes,' he says, in a non-committal tone. I wait for him to say something more, but he just watches me.

'The last lot of therapy really helped, I think. It sorted things out, and ever since then everything's been fine.'

Dr Goldman nods expressionlessly. I wish he would ask me something.

'So ... these headaches I've been having, as I told you on the phone ... my mother had them, too, a lot of the time, when I was a kid. I've been on medication but, you know, you've got to watch out with these things. It's easy to get hooked ...' I trail off helplessly.

'Do you feel you are becoming addicted?' Dr Goldman asks.

'No.'

'Then how can I help?'

I stare at him for a while. What am I supposed to say?

'Well, I told Wendy I would come ... we had an argument at the kids' sports day. It was stupid, really. I was wrong, I can see that. Sometimes I just want so much for the kids, maybe I push a little bit too hard. But it's better than not taking any interest at all, surely.'

Dr Goldman nods, and watches me. I feel uncomfortable with the silence.

'Do you mind if I take some notes?' he asks. I nod, yes.

'I mean, coming second is good,' I say. 'But you need someone to tell you that you can come first. I want my kids to know that I believe in them. I also want them to know that they can achieve anything if they work hard and are committed to it. My father never told me that. I had to learn it for myself. I was a late bloomer. I could have done much more if I had realised my potential from the beginning.'

'So your father did not help you enough?'

'No,' I say. 'I'm not blaming him for anything. It's just an observation, that's all.'

Again, silence. To fill up the space I start telling him about my obsession with cricket. Suddenly, as I am telling the story, I feel as if I am outside the scene, observing this child practising day and night with his cricket bat, and coming home with that one little mention in the cricket club annual, underlined in blue pen. And I see my father turning away, and his soft, expressionless voice saying, 'They'd never pick a Jew.' I feel sorry for that child, and I feel something else, too. I watch the man turning away, and I feel something wrenching up from below. I become aware that Dr Goldman is sitting opposite, watching me. His solicitous expression irritates me. My face is wet, and my cheeks are stinging. I feel nauseous. And my head is throbbing like it is going to burst. I am suddenly furious to be stuck in this ridiculous position.

'There are some tissues behind you.' Dr Goldman says. He points towards the shelf.

When I have swabbed the tears off my face, I say, 'I'm sorry, I guess I'm just overwrought. It's the headaches, they've really upset me.'

'No,' Dr Goldman says, unexpectedly. 'I don't think it is just the headaches.'

'What do you mean?'

'We need some more time to explore this. Perhaps you should make another appointment.'

'How long will it take?' I say. 'I can't wait around for years.'

'I don't know,' he says. 'We could begin next week.'

'Well, can I expect some improvement in … let's say … six weeks?'

Dr Goldman stares at me calmly.

'I'll have to think about it,' I say. 'I've got a lot of commitments at the moment.'

'Well,' he says, 'that's up to you. But this time next week is available.'

I want to say, 'But there's nothing wrong with me.' But that seems stupid. So I say, 'I can't make a commitment now.'

'Okay,' he says. 'It's up to you.'

I leave, and apologise again for the emotional scene. He just nods, and says, 'Ring me during the week to let me know what you've decided.'

As I pass the picture in the waiting room, I notice the people without faces, and I just want to be out of there as quickly as possible, never to return. I am sure that if I make one more effort of will I can force these problems to recede, as I have done before. It's too easy to be distracted by these messy, emotional issues. If I just focus on work, family, my own small world, I'm sure things will sort themselves out. As I walk out of the door of the building, under the wrought-iron balcony, I am one hundred per cent convinced I will never cross that threshold again.

Laws and Journeys

My accountancy office is a haven of orderliness. The piles of papers on my desk, filled with figures—figures that add up neatly into firm columns and unshakeable totals, with elegant and satisfying precision—are the things that matter in life. The folders, sheets, and faxes that pile up hour after hour in the in-tray are saying to me: You are a success. Your life is clear, straightforward. They also say: Here is what you will be doing tomorrow. Here is what you will think about next week, and the following week, and in six months' time. It will all be here, like the secretaries and the mahogany conference table, and the clients, and my accountancy certificate on the wall. None of it will change. No surprises.

I take Wendy out on a drive to Daylesford: all afternoon we look at antiques, chat about everyday things, eat dinner in a restaurant overlooking the lake. I am quite sure that I have restored a sense of normalcy, without resorting to the good doctor. Wendy is calm, smiling, her spirits lightened.

'I'm glad you're so much better,' Wendy says. 'The doctor must really have helped.'

'Well, the doctor didn't do very much, really,' I say. 'It's just a question of willpower.'

'Well,' she says, 'that's something you've always had a lot of.' I am not sure whether that comment is a little ironic, but I ignore that.

'Yes,' I continue. 'It's just willpower.'

Wendy doesn't say anything. She just looks out over the lake, which is a clear grey sheet in the twilight.

As I eat the smoked salmon and drink the sauvignon blanc, I feel again the comforting blanket of success drawn around me and my family. After all, there is nothing that routine and effort cannot resolve. I am quit of pain and the past. No shadows. I am myself once again, a good husband, a good father, an important man. I feel full of life.

'How about we take the kids skiing next week?' I say. 'For my birthday weekend.'

'You go,' Wendy says. 'You know I hate the cold. I'll have a weekend by myself.'

'Okay, I say. I'll ask John Weisman if he wants to go.'

'Yes, go with John. It'll be a good break. As long as you're really feeling better.'

'One hundred per cent,' I say confidently.

Over the following weeks I throw myself compulsively into the lives of my children. I'm there shouting hoarsely as Amy's basketball team leaps to victory. I spur Rachel on as she sprints around the running track. On parent-teacher night I make sure that I see every single teacher, and throw them a few googlies to make sure that they are doing their jobs properly. I am glad to hear that the kids are doing well, and I bask in the sense of achievement. I'm lucky that I know how to be a good father. If my father was no help in anything else, at least he taught me to be the opposite of everything that he was. And my kids bear that out. They are happy and confident, the teachers say. All in all, I am very satisfied with the school—it may be expensive, but I am determined that my children will have everything I never had myself.

My birthday comes and goes, and on the following Saturday I get up early and run around like a man possessed, checking the skiing gear, finishing up things at work. There are a hundred-and-one last-minute arrangements to make before we can set off. Then, in the morning, I remember with irritation that I have a *barmitzvah* to go to.

'It's not something I can avoid,' I tell Wendy. 'It's the son of one of my clients.'

'I can't possibly come right now,' Wendy says. 'I have to get the girls ready. You should have told me before.'

'I have to make an appearance,' I say. 'It'll only be an hour or so, at the most. They can pack the bags ready to go.'

I arrive rather late, out of breath from the rush. I watch the people around me; men in suits and women in hats. From near the back of the synagogue I watch the young boy seated on the front bench, as the cantor recites the Hebrew *parashah*, the weekly reading from the Torah. I close my eyes and listen like a child, hearing the roll and fall of a language I cannot understand. Instead, I just listen to the sounds. The guttural consonants catch the throat like the dry wind of the desert. The lisping phrases run together like the entreaties of a lover. The vowels seem long and dark, unable to give up their mourning for some distant loss. I listen for a long time to the singing notes of the cantor, up and down. It is mournful, and at the same time trembling with life, like an unbearable, quivering note from a violin. I mean only to stay for a few minutes because there are still things to do before we leave at midday. But slowly the singing makes me forget the checklist of things to do which is running through my mind. I stay a moment longer.

All at once, the language touches me with a shock. I look around to see if the rest of the congregation is reacting, expecting to see at least the scrolls spilling forth from the tabernacle, and the black-clothed men pushing toward the doorway. But no, nothing has happened, except that the young boy, the *barmitzvah*, has risen to read from the Torah. His lips move, gathering speed and confidence in the unfamiliar reading. And then suddenly, inexplicably, I find that I can understand. I miss a lot of words and phrases, but I can comprehend most of them. Sometimes I can even race ahead of the words to anticipate what is coming. I look down at the paper I picked up when I came in. The *parashah* that the mitzvah is reading is the same one that I read in this synagogue at my own *barmitzvah*, just after my own thirteenth birthday more than three decades ago.

Outside, a bright, cloudless winter day is shining over Melbourne, and I remember my car packed full with skis and thick padded jackets and woollen sweaters. And I try to think of the days ahead. I try to think of the freedom and the wind, the children jumping in the snow, and the lifts tilting upward to the sky. I try to think of the road I will take towards the mountains, comparing the relative distances of different routes and debating their merits in my head. I try to focus on the reason I am here. I search for my client—he is sitting near the *bimah*, listening to his son reciting the ancient text. I note down mentally a few details to discuss with him the next time I see him. Looking at his back, I wonder what his thoughts are. Then, for a moment, he turns to his wife, and I try to see his face. Somehow I can't focus properly. I notice that he has taken his wife's hand, and he is gripping it tightly. He cranes his head around to look at the congregation. His face, normally so stolid and businesslike, is flushed with a strange excitement, a look of ownership and humility at once. It is not a look I recognise. In his survey of the room he notices me standing near the door, and gives me a grateful nod. It is odd to see him beaming so broadly, given his usual sober, rather reserved manner.

My presence having been duly noted, I can easily leave now. It is curiously difficult to drag myself from this warm, humming room into the cold air outside, but I do. I walk to the car, my breath puffing mouthfuls of white fog into the air. I drive the packed car home to pick up the kids. Then I stop at John's house, and we set out on the drive north towards the mountains.

As we drive, I talk to John about business, the committees we work on, his work as a barrister. He is telling me about the case he has been working on for the past few years, a major lawsuit with implications for the future of the country. I watch him as he speaks, and I admire his confidence, his success. I make a comment here and there, and he nods, or smiles at my observations. His way of speaking is economical, always carefully judged. He doesn't waste words. I am lucky to have such a friend. I am proud to be accepted by him as an equal, to be flying along the road into the mountains, watching fields and hills pass by as the frosts on the fields become thicker, and the terrain more rocky.

As he talks, I find myself losing a sentence here and there. I am trying to concentrate.

'Are you feeling okay?' he asks.

'Fine,' I say. 'Sorry, I was just watching the road. What was that last bit you were saying?' He repeats the story. The white stripes passing to my right seem to be beating out a rhythm. In between the stripes, the words of the *parashah* are turning in my head, set loose from their moorings and dancing along the road ahead of me, waiting around corners, and vanishing away into the cold air. The words are thumping louder in my head, and the white stripes on the road are giving me a headache.

'Excuse me a second, John.' I say. I turn the mirror so I can see Amy and Rachel horsing around in the back of the car.

'Amy,' I say.

'Yes, Dad?'

'Did you see my white bag? Did you put it in the car? The little one on the dining table.'

'Rachel picked up all the bags that were left,' she says.

'No I didn't,' Rachel says, poking Amy in the side.

'Amy, I asked you to look after the bags,' I say. She is not listening. She is pushing Rachel back. 'Amy!' I say, sharply.

'What, Dad?' she says. Rachel is giggling helplessly.

'Stop it, Rachel!' I say. 'Right now! Amy, the white bag on the dining table.'

'What white bag?' she asks.

'Oh, I can't believe it!' I say. I pull the car into a turn-off on the side of the road.

'What's wrong? What have you lost?' John asks.

'I'm really sorry, John,' I say as I open the door. 'It's the bag with my tablets in it. I'm sure it got left behind. I can't do without it. We might have to go back. What a pain.'

I go round to the back of the car and start pulling out the bags onto the frosty ground. John waits in the car for a minute or so, then he gets out and walks over to me.

'I'm so sorry,' I say. 'Everything's ruined. I can't believe it, the one thing I don't do myself …'

John looks into the back, moves things aside and picks up the bag.

'This one?' he says.

I stand there for a while, staring at the bag.

'Perhaps I can drive for a while,' he says.

'No, really, I'm fine' I say. I shut the boot, and walk toward the front of the car. My legs feel unsteady beneath me. 'Maybe you're right,' I say. 'I'm not feeling all that great.'

'Sure,' John says. I walk over to give him the keys. I feel dizzy.

'Would you mind if I walk along the road for a minute,' I say. 'I feel sick.'

'Of course,' he says. He sits in the driver's seat and talks to the girls.

I open the white bag, and take a couple of tablets, then walk down the road a little way, out of sight of the car. Around me the hills are covered in white.

I remember myself as a twelve-year-old boy in 1962, standing at the gate of a house with a verandah and red-brick fence, opening the gate and walking along the curving path to a recessed doorway. I reached out hesitantly to knock on the dark wood of the door. I waited, for what seemed a long time. I narrowed my eyes, but it was hard to see far into the dim window next to the door. I could see only the reflection of a rather thin, nervous child. I waited uncertainly for several minutes and almost turning to go before the sound of creaking floorboards made my heart pound again. The door swung open to reveal a man much younger than I had expected—tall, with eyes a little red from concentration. At once he took me by the arm and led me in, saying, 'Ah, you don't have to knock, just waltz right in, make yourself at home.' And he waved me to follow him into the gloomy hallway. 'I'll just move some books,' he said. Inside, the house was crammed like a warehouse up to its high Edwardian ceilings with books, more than I'd ever seen in one place, bound volumes and pamphlets, scrolls and bundles of loose pages, most of them in foreign languages and scripts I couldn't decipher. It was as though some great tide of words had rolled out of a distant sea, and broken over this green Melbourne suburb, fetching a cargo of flotsam up in this room with its picture-rails and peeling wallpaper.

Rabbi Levi sat me down on a worn-looking leather couch, and disappeared for some time. He came back into the room carrying some books which he set down, and picked up others, and felt around for his spectacles, and finally sat down beside me. 'You're Marin, yes? Bernard, from Stanislaw?' I'd never heard my father called by that name before. He was always Stan. But I nodded all the same. 'Good,' he said. 'We'll start from the start, yes?'

'Okay,' I said. 'Please.'

When I left the rabbi's gloomy book-crammed citadel, I felt that strange, incense-scented mysteries had begun to open about me. Walking home along the familiar streets, I wondered what all of this had to do with my cricket-playing, tropical fish-breeding life as an Australian boy. Would I be leaving forever the carefree, material existence that I had enjoyed? Would all these songs and hymns and commentaries of five thousand years make me into a different kind of human being? I was suddenly conscious as I'd never been before that my world was made up of Jews, and others who were not Jews, and this troubled me more than learning to read a Hebrew text, or standing up before the synagogue to make the journey into manhood.

I began to ask questions I had never asked before. Though Paul and I had attended Jewish Sunday School, and picked up a smattering of religious knowledge from the undisciplined lessons, I, like most of the other boys, had never considered this anything more than an unfortunate necessity to be disposed of as quickly and with as little fuss as possible. I had heard my father discussing religion with his friends from time to time, and I wondered if this might be a subject on which he could advise and direct me. Perhaps it offered a way back to my father.

When Passover came, the ritual of *seder* and family gatherings, I looked around at my family, and began for the first time to see the edges of the Jewish world in which I'd always lived. My mother's relations formed a large, tight-knit Jewish family—my mum's father Nathan and his wife Sabina, his sister Leah and his brother Leon, and their husbands, wives, and families. My father, too, was part of this clan, since he and my mother were first cousins—his mother was Nathan's sister. Yet they never really seemed like my father's family. Everyone was removed one step from him, since those closest to him had stayed behind in Poland when he was sent alone to a new land. And they disappeared with the rest of those left behind. We never mentioned these missing, shadowy figures—his parents, his brothers and sisters. I knew vaguely that they had existed, perhaps even heard their names. But somehow a veil had been drawn over them. Occasionally, the talk over the family table began to drift towards the past, towards the Warsaw of my father's youth. Then the conversation would fall away into silence, as though something cast a black shadow in the way of the past.

Despite these strange, unexplained absences, this clan of cousins and uncles and aunts and grandparents had always clung around me like a seamless fabric, connected by familiar streets and houses which were second homes and backyards I knew from fence to fence. But now, as the first glimmer of history dawned upon me, I began to see that this little city of my own existed inside a much bigger world, in which my family was only a tiny corner.

We spent Passover night at the home of Nellie Goldberg, my mother's cousin. Her husband, Urisz, was a religious man who attended the synagogue regularly and observed all the ritual of the high holy days. I watched him carefully all evening. With the little Hebrew I had learned from Rabbi Levi, I strained to understand something of the prayers he was reciting. After the meal, I asked Nellie what he was saying, but she shushed me with, 'He's just *davening*'. I watched him with rapt interest as he shook and murmured.

'What does it mean?' I asked.

'It is *Hallel*,' she said. 'The story of the Exodus from Egypt.'

Urisz stopped and turned to me.

'You should have learned these things already,' he said. 'Learn your Hebrew. Learn to ask the questions. It is part of Haggadah tradition. In Torah, it says, "In time to come, when your son asks, 'What does this mean?' you shall say to him, 'With mighty hand the Lord brought us out from Egypt, the house of bondage.'" You should know all of this.'

Urisz turned back to his praying, the guttural consonants and chanting vowels of his Hebrew. Then the insistent rhythm of the prayer shook and faltered. Another loud recitation was coming from the other side of the room. It took a moment to recognise that it was my father's voice. He was sitting at the table. In a loud voice, he was reciting the winners of the daily double and the trifecta from Saturday's *Sporting Globe*. He read the winners and placegetters, the starting prices, and the totalisator payouts down to pounds, shillings, and pence. Urisz stopped praying, and I watched him, aghast at what would happen next.

My father read on and on, while Urisz simply stood in the middle of the floor with an indescribable look on his face. After a while, my father finished reading the page, and folded up the paper. He got up to go. As he walked past, Urisz said, 'You bring shame on this house.' He spat out the words like a curse. My father stopped and looked at him.

'It won't help anyone,' he said. 'It's all rubbish. We are living in Australia now. You should give it up.'

'You are a Jew,' Urisz said, excitedly, then pointed to me. 'Your son is a Jew. And he knows nothing of his people.'

My father just shrugged contemptuously.

'What is there to know?' he said. 'All this muttering and ranting? All your backward, selfish ideas? Your jealous God?' He shook his head. 'There is no God, so forget it.'

'You abandon your own people?' Urisz replied, his voice rising in pitch. 'You abandon God? It is said, "The twig that falls from the tree must wither away. The leaf that falls must dry up." He shook his fist in my father's face. 'You are the selfish one. You bring a curse on yourself. You bring a curse on your family.'

He was gesturing at my father, pointing accusingly with his finger. I saw the flush of anger rising into my father's face, and, for a moment, I wondered if he would strike Urisz. There was a ghastly silence. Nellie and my mother had come from the other room. My mother rushed forward and seemed about to take my father's arm and pull him away. But her hand just touched his arm lightly and fell back. Then he seemed to sink into himself, as though shrinking an inch or two into his shoes. He exhaled painfully as though he had been holding his breath. Then he opened his paper again and walked away. I looked down at the floor, pretending that I wasn't there, that I had not witnessed this ugly scene. No-one spoke of it again—it lapsed back into a habitual tense silence.

The following week I crept guiltily into the rabbi's house, like an impostor waiting to be unmasked and cast out of the ranks of the faithful. I thought about Urisz's words, *The twig that falls from the tree must wither away. The leaf that falls must dry up.* The rabbi must find out my father is an atheist, I thought, and I will arrive on the verandah one day to find the door bolted against me. But if the rabbi knew he never made a sign, and the lessons continued, week after week, no longer a mysterious adventure but now an unpleasant necessity. And as my thirteenth birthday came and went, and the day of *barmitzvah* approached, I began to dread that something awful would happen at the ceremony. Would my father perform his part in the ceremony? Would he demonstrate his contempt for religion as he had at Nellie's? Would he embarrass me so badly that I would want to run out of the synagogue and never return? Over and over I tried to think of a way to avoid the impending catastrophe—and this, rather than the guiding words of Rabbi Levi, was what occupied my thoughts while I sat among the books and papers and tried to learn to be a Jew.

But somehow, with no gift and little concentration, I still learned to read my *parashah*. I wound a slow and halting path among the strange and difficult letters. And when the appointed day arrived my father sat quietly beside me at the synagogue, his face expressionless, whether in disgust or indifference I could not tell. When the time came for him to open the curtains of the ark he rose shyly and performed his part self-consciously, as though he was uncomfortable in front of the congregation. The rabbi began to speak, and as I saw that my father was not about to leave me covered in shame and embarrassment, I began to listen as his soft voice drifted over me like a sleep and a beginning.

The rabbi explained the meaning of the reading, *Matot—Masei*, Laws and Journeys, from the Book of Numbers, the fourth of the five books of the Pentateuch. He spoke of the wanderings of the Israelites who left the cruelties of Egypt for the deserts of Sinai, and the long and arduous years under the leadership of Moses and Aaron his brother. The rabbi's tongue tripped familiarly over the exotic names: Succoth and Etham, Migdol, Pi-hahiroth and Marah. The Israelites wandered on, past the twelve springs and seventy palm trees of Elim, past the Sea of Reeds, and Hazeroth and Libnah, Mount Shepher, and the wilderness of Kadesh. On and on they went, for forty years, until they reached the Jordan, the boundary of the land of Canaan. Then the rabbi spoke of the laws and commands given from the Lord to the people of Israel by their prophet—the vows and rules which were the foundation of survival, in a time when human life was forfeit to the laws of a violent, inhuman law. The Lord commanded the people of Israel to slay the Midianites—not only their men, but all of the married women, too. I looked at my father, as though I might find some clue to these strange and horrible events.

My father's face was very far away from this warm and comforting synagogue. The calm voice of the rabbi curled around the heads of women in elaborate hats, drifted past groups of boys jostling at the back, and men adjusting the folds of their tallis or gathering in small clusters outside. I was no longer really listening. His voice was beating out the moments until I would rise and read, and become a man, a Jew. I would be someone who could make up a *minyan* in the synagogue for the reading of prayers, and sip the wine of celebration while reciting the *kiddush*.

The rabbi gestured to me, and I walked up alone to the raised platform. I looked back at my father. He had a tight-lipped smile fixed on his face. His eyes were turned downwards. I began to read the words of the Torah, falling into the rhythm of what I had learned. The rabbi smiled encouragingly. I began the *haphtara*, the prophetic reading from Jeremiah which was affixed to my *parashah*.

'Then said I, Ah, Lord God! behold,' I read, painstakingly, 'I cannot speak; for I am a child. But the Lord said unto me, Say not, I am a child; for thou shalt go to all that I send thee, and whatsoever I command thee, thou shalt speak.' I watched my father's face for a sign that he heard, that he cared, that he was part of my journey to manhood. But his features were more indecipherable than the branched and swooping characters which cut like scythes of black ink across the page before me. 'The word of the Lord came unto me, saying, "What do you see?" And I said, "I see a rod of an almond tree."' Slowly, I watched my father turn his eyes down and stare at his hands. As I read, I waited for some sign that he was part of this event, but it never came. My eyes were stinging, and my reading began to falter. The rabbi laid his arm on my shoulder and closed the book. I remember nothing more of the service after that—just a feeling of dull, thick silence, darkened at its edges.

After the service, my family and friends gathered at our house for the subdued celebration which was all our deteriorating finances could afford. I thought of what the rabbi had taught me in that room full of books and peeling wallpaper. Only one out of the thousands of things he had said had stuck in my mind. *Baruch she-petarani*, he sang to me in Hebrew, wagging his eyebrows at me to translate. It is the traditional Talmudic prayer of a father at the *barmitzvah* of his son. 'Blessed is He who has freed me from the responsibility of this child.'

I walk back to the car, and John is waiting quietly, talking to the girls. I get in on the passenger side.

'How are you feeling?' he asks. 'Better?'

'It was nothing,' I say. 'Just a headache.'

He starts up the car, and turns back onto the road.

I try to talk normally, and forget about the scenes replaying in my head. I keep the conversation focused on our mutual interests: business, the law, the committees on which we serve. I mention a friend who has taken time off.

'Yes, it comes thick and fast sometimes,' John says. 'It's a bit hard to take when it all comes at once.'

'But you, you're always on top of all that stuff,' I say. 'You always get things done.'

The tablet is beginning to work, and my headache is receding slightly.

'Well,' he says, 'lately, it hasn't been so easy.'

'With the High Court case?'

'No,' he says. 'I don't mean that. I haven't been well.'

I know that he has suffered from health problems since his childhood. I've always admired the way he has never allowed these problems to hold him back in his career. I will do the same thing, I think. I will do whatever it takes to get rid of these headaches and move on.

'You'll pull through, as usual,' I say. 'You always do.'

I look across at him and I think what a different man this is from my father, someone one can trust and admire, a true role model. My father only hid behind his illnesses. But John has never let such things get in his way.

'I'll take a leaf out of your book,' I say. 'I really have to do something about these headaches.'

'Yes,' John says. 'You should.'

I think about Dr Goldman, and I decide that he is, after all, my best hope. I will make a firm arrangement with him as soon as I return. Whatever it takes to rid me of these headaches, I will do it.

I look over at John. He is watching the road in front of us. For a moment, the faraway look on his face seems very familiar.

'So,' I say. 'Tell me some more about this High Court case.'

He seems to summon himself back with an effort. We drive on, talking about things of importance, things that I know about, that hold no dark shadows. And after a while, the words of the *barmitzvah* are forgotten again, and the white lines on the road are just white lines again.

The Letter

'Six weeks,' I say. 'That's the way I'm thinking about it.' I'm sitting on the couch in Dr Goldman's consulting room a week after the ski trip. He looks at me, and waits for me to continue.

'I'm committing myself to that,' I say. 'But I expect to get rid of the headaches at least.'

'It isn't very long,' he says. 'But maybe long enough to make a start.'

'A start?' I say. 'I can't sit around forever. You told me that a course of therapy would make a difference.'

'No, I said we need to make a start, and then see where that takes us.'

'Well, I'm telling you that my main priority is to get rid of these headaches.'

'It's possible the headaches are only a symptom.'

'What are you saying? That I need more tests?'

'It's not necessarily an organic cause. There's something you started talking about last time. About your father. Perhaps you could continue'

'Oh, that. It isn't really all that important.'

'Tell me more about your relationship.'

'My relationship? I didn't have a relationship with him.'

Once again, Dr Goldman watches me calmly. We sit in silence for quite a while, and I feel that I'm wasting time. So, to use the hour more effectively, I begin to tell the story of the *barmitzvah*. As I am talking, the doctor stops me and tells me the time is up. I am surprised to have spoken for so long, and I find myself waiting to finish the story the following week.

When I get to the end, I try to describe the look on my father's face as he opened the curtains of the ark. I realise that I cannot remember.

'What was he thinking?' I say. 'I have no idea.'

Dr Goldman doesn't reply.

'He was completely cold. He felt nothing at all.'

I sit and think for a minute.

'No, I'm sorry, that's not true … Look, I just don't know what he felt,' I say. 'Actually, I think he felt proud of me. Yes, I'm sure he must have been proud of me.'

Suddenly I am convinced.

'You feel he was proud of you.' Dr Goldman repeats my words back to me.

'Well, he must have been, mustn't he? He wasn't a bad father. I know that.'

I don't say anything for a while. Dr Goldman is watching me, and I am wondering what he sees. I wonder if I'm crazy. I wonder what he wants me to say. I try to think about something else.

'He wasn't a bad father,' I say the following week. 'He fought in World War Two, you know. But he didn't talk about it.'

I start to tell another story, one which I have not thought about for many years.

In a handful of mail, mostly bills addressed to my father, and some local circulars for my mother, the protruding edge of a long white envelope turned my stomach like sour milk. In the right-hand corner was the black insignia of the Department of Labour and National Service. It was burned into the stiff cartridge paper like a brand. I took the mail into the house and handed my parents their letters. Everything looked much the same as it had every day for the twenty years of my life. My mother was busy with the endless routine which prevented her from looking up or asking questions about her life, chasing the dust from the cushions and rugs with characteristic single-mindedness. My father was sitting in front of the television, neither awake nor asleep, but in some nether world of his own, like a character left out of a story. Only the absence of Paul left our picture of silent unhappiness incomplete. He had left for Tasmania, trying to jump-start the law degree which had stalled badly in the past few years, like all of our lives.

I took the letter to my room and stared at it for a long time, as though perhaps it would vanish with the same suddenness as it had come. I didn't need to open it. Just the black, featureless typeface of my name, printed across the face of the envelope, spelled out a long, dreaded, intolerable sentence. Between the letters, I could breathe the bitter smoke of the Vietnamese sky, full of the smell of blood and cordite; the blades of the helicopters rolling over the mud-hut villages; the crater-scarred fields; children running; bodies scattered along the sides of rivers. I tried to imagine myself a part of this, over and over again. I tried to find a part of my being that was not revolted by this senseless chaos. I would stand up, and steel myself to open the letter. I would simply close my eyes and let the machine of war swallow me up. I thought of my father, smiling quietly, confidently, in his digger's uniform, risking his life to defend his country and his family. But I could not stand long enough before nausea swept through me again. I thought about my friends, the intense, passionate anti-war protesters and their rock-hard certainty that the war was wrong and unjust. I snatched up the letter again, in a sudden fierce determination to tear it up without reading it. But as I bent the stiff packet in the middle, I saw the life of hiding and running that stood ahead of me, the humiliating, degrading shadow of prison. I knew that some people had made that choice, and given everything to their cause. But I didn't want to be a hero. I just wanted to stop this from happening. I was very frightened.

That evening, at dinner, I stared at my food with a pale, washed-out feeling of unreality. I said nothing to my parents, as though by not acknowledging the sharp fact it might somehow turn out not to be true. Suddenly I wanted their boring, stifling, suburban routine to wrap around me like a cloud and hide me from the ugly, terrifying reality into which I'd been suddenly thrown. I needed desperately to find some kind of anchor to the ground, something that could not be blown away by these remorseless winds. I needed help to find a path through the chaos. I looked at my father quietly chewing the meat my mother always cut up into small pieces for him since his illness. I remembered the photograph of him in his army uniform that sat on the mantel. He knows about these things, I thought. For once, he can help me. I steeled myself to ask him a direct question.

'Dad,' I said, my voice sounding hollow in the quietness of the room, 'can I ask you something?'

I stopped. The silence was thicker than before. I started again, awkwardly. 'I got a letter from the National Service. My number came up.'

Slowly, he put down his fork. He stared at me for a long time, with an indescribable look on his face.

'You were in the war. I thought you could help me.'

He seemed to go pale. He looked down, picked up his fork and continued to eat in silence. I tried again.

'I know it was different in those days—there was a good reason to fight,' I ventured. 'And I would have done the same thing.'

'You don't know what you're talking about,' he said, in a low voice, without looking up.

'It's not the same thing with Vietnam. It's wrong.'

My father looked up. 'All war is wrong,' he said, quietly, and began eating again.

'But Dad,' I said, 'you told me yourself that this war in Vietnam is a mistake. This time we're the ones who are doing the killing.'

My father looked at me, as though he wanted to say something but did not know how to begin.

'I feel like we're doing the same thing. When people supported Hitler …'

He stood up. 'That's it,' he shouted. He banged his fist on the table. 'Don't talk about things you know nothing about.' All the blood had rushed to his face. He seemed about to bang the table again, then stopped in mid-motion. He just stood there, veins bulging in his temples, his arm protruding like the branch of a dead tree. After a few moments his colour returned to normal, and his arm fell to his side. He met my mother's gaze, and she looked down at the table and began clearing the dishes. He mastered himself with an effort, mumbling a little, and sat down again.

I sat for a little while, I don't know how long, just staring at my plate, and then I got up and left the room. My mother came after me, and stood in the doorway of my bedroom.

'You didn't eat anything, Bernard,' she said.

I walked past her without speaking, and left the house, carrying the unopened letter with me.

'My father was a cunt.'

I hear this coming out of my mouth, and I am shocked. I would like to make a joke, cover it up, leave the building.

'He was a fucking bastard,' I say.

Dr Goldman sits in silence for a long time. After a while, I realise that it is really I who have just spoken. For a moment I had wondered if someone else was in the room. I don't say anything for a long time. Dr Goldman is silent also. After ten minutes or so the session is over, and I leave.

Max

During the week I anticipate my next session anxiously, as though I need to finish telling the story I have begun. At last, the week comes around, and I am back in Dr Goldman's office, with the roll-top desk and the couch. Almost before I have greeted him I begin the story again. I want to tell him about Max, my mother's cousin—the only person I felt could help me in this crisis.

I left my parents' house with the envelope containing my fate clutched in my hand. I walked and walked, all the way to Balaclava, and knocked on the door of Max's apartment. There was no answer. I sat down on the step in front of the door, my eyes stinging with disappointment. I thought about the times we'd spent together in the past few years. I remembered one day in particular, walking along the winding path around the lake at the Botanical Gardens. Beside me, with his camera held in the palm of his hand, and his eyes darting from side to side in search of the perfect image—a fallen tree, a black swan ruffling its plumage, fruit bats sleeping upside-down in the shady heights of the palms—was Max. He was more than thirty years my senior, but could still at times wear me out with his frenzied, apparently inexhaustible interest in the world. He tore off up the grassy slope near the lake, turning and running backwards with his camera held to his eye, shouting to me to follow him up, waving his free arm madly. I raced up the hill, trying to run diagonally across the hill to avoid the line of his picture, but wherever I ran I couldn't get out of his camera range. He was waving and shouting at me from the top of the hill. At last I reached him, panting breathlessly and sweating from the exertion.

'Sorry, Max,' I said. 'I guess I ruined your shot.'

'You're a real idiot,' he said. 'I was trying to get a picture of you.'

It had never really occurred to me until that moment that anyone, let alone this man, so much older and wiser than me, could think of me as anything but a burden, to be tolerated only because of my inability to fend for myself. Unlike this figure in his jaunty light-grey suit and Homberg hat, who would bound through the world with a light, confident step, I felt heavy weights as I struggled through the world. It seemed to me that wherever I turned there were obstacles and difficulties. The five years since I had turned sixteen in 1966 had seen a catastrophic change in my demeanour. I was no longer the dynamic rover on the football field darting in and out of the packs, or the slips fieldsman and wicket keeper with lightning reflexes. I stopped playing sport altogether. My schoolwork, too, degenerated alarmingly. I became quiet, introverted, and shy. I lost my self-esteem, and grew self-conscious and felt estranged from my friends.

Watching my decline, my father only expressed a distant regret which at times seemed like indifference and at others like disappointment. 'You carry the weight of the world on your shoulders, Bernard,' he would remark. But his detachment from my life, like a tourist passing through on his way somewhere else, was part of the burden which was pulling my shoulders into a stoop, curving my spine, and leaving me conscious of the first faint lines on my teenage brow. Some unspoken downturn had clearly occurred in his life also. He took less interest in the world at large with each day that passed, and his financial situation was rapidly deteriorating along with his health. My mother began working in an office to make up the shortfall, and sometimes I heard them arguing about his careless largesse, which demonstrated his lack of interest in money and the future. He made no obvious effort to change things, preferring instead to drift along in a mist of preoccupation, dull routine, and occasional unmotivated outbursts of irritation.

But then there was Max, the only friend I managed to keep during this time. My father was fading deeper into the background, like the poorly fixed colour snapshots of the sixties. But Max was bursting into life on both sides of the camera. I found myself increasingly in Max's company, more as a result of his indomitable magnanimity than from any faithfulness on my part. Max was everything my father was not—bohemian, artistic, and expansive. There was never a situation that left him at a loss for a joke, an anecdote. His speech was peppered with spicy Yiddishisms from his days in the Kadimah Jewish theatre in Carlton, and pieces of business acumen picked up during his life in the rag trade. He had run a fashion house in Flinders Lane, crammed into a labyrinthine Victorian edifice along with tailors and furriers, seamstresses in sweatshops, wigmakers, and a floor that churned out all manner of prosthetic limbs. His stories were a strange breath from a world which he, like so many others among the denizens of the twisting inner-city lanes, left behind in Eastern Europe—magical, enchanting, filled with mystery, romance, and danger.

Max possessed a baroque sense of the wonderful and grotesque. A succession of the still rather provincial Australian women of the 1960s fell prey to his indomitable European charm. His one great tragedy—which he did not conceal but rather complained of with considerable vigour and frequency—was his German wife, Susie, with whom he lived unhappily for twenty years. Since they had no children, it was difficult to say why they stayed together. At moments I could not help but wonder if she provided the background that set off his pearls of witty conversation. But despite his marital woes and his reckless philandering, his childless state seemed to touch him more deeply than any of his other griefs and passions.

Through my teenage years I found his company more and more pleasant. At large family gatherings, he in turn would gravitate towards his two young cousins who delighted in the stories that others had certainly heard many times over. And Paul and I enjoyed the novel sense that our ideas, thoughts, and feelings were in some way valuable and interesting. He seemed genuinely intrigued by our world, by Bob Dylan and Woodstock, the Vietnam Moratorium and the Chicago Seven. As time passed we gradually became fixtures of one another's lives—one of those gradual adoptions which creep up until they seem they have always been there.

At last, one day—perhaps that day in the Botanical Gardens, or later that afternoon, helping him to develop the shots he'd taken from the hill, my anxious face emerging slowly in the milky solution—suddenly, I felt that I had a father after all. Not that silent, fading figure who had brought me into the world and now seemed so intent on disappearing from it, but this extraordinary man, painted in bright, contrasting colours like the landscapes and mythical scenes we studied together at Montsalvat and Heide. This was a character full of the crazy Jewish brilliance of the Marx Brothers films I adored, someone who embraced my furtive passion for graffiti as a form of self-expression, laughing delightedly at my confessions. Someone who loved me like a son.

I was still sitting on the step, holding the envelope in my hand. At last I got up to go. But suddenly there was a muffled click, and Max opened the door a crack and looked out. He was in his dressing gown. I was overjoyed to find him there after all, and I jumped up and burst through the door into the room and hugged him. He, on the other hand, was a little nonplussed to find me sitting there on his doorstep. He stood for a while staring at me, and then he suddenly burst into raucous laughter.

'It's okay, Joycie, c'mon out.' he yelled. 'It's just my crazy cousin.'

A somewhat bedraggled woman in her late forties emerged from the bedroom. She had the buxom fullness of a woman who had once been striking, independent, and appealing. There still remained something racy and compelling about her—perhaps her gravelly voice, the little feathery adjustments she made to her blowsy exterior, or the broad grin, edged with ruby lipstick, which she flashed as she put out her hand, using the other to hold her bathrobe closed.

'Joyce Crickstead, meet Bernard Marin,' Max said, laughing.

'Sorry, darl,' Joyce said to me, smiling cheekily as she shook my hand.

They both listened with sympathy to my problems. 'You know, we used to have that problem back in Europe,' he said. He told me how, in Poland and Russia, young Jewish men would ulcerate their legs to avoid being conscripted into the army.

'But here it's so much better, best country in the world,' he said. 'They're nothing but a bunch of *schlemiels*. You only need a rash.'

Within a couple of days, through some contacts in the peace network, I found a doctor who showed me how to produce the dermatological symptoms I would need to fail the army medical. When the examining medical officer saw the red, inflamed skin on my knees and elbows, and heard my carefully rehearsed story of incessant itching and discomfort, he frowned silently. Watching his face, I knew that the panic was over, and I would never have to fight in this interminable war, far away from my family, friends, and the comforts of home.

Home

The six weeks of my therapy with Dr Goldman are almost over. It's almost spring. The days seem colder, and the bare twigs of the oaks and beeches planted along the suburban avenues have not yet begun to bud, overlooked by the tall, dry eucalypts. I'm on my way to pick Mum up for a doctor's appointment. My mother still lives in the same house in North Road, Ormond, where she and my father spent the four decades of their married life. I haven't been there for some time—she's been overseas visiting a friend, or maybe a relative: the two are always mixed up in our family. I arrive at the house early, and she's not home. So I let myself in and wander around the house waiting for her to come back from her errand. I look at the furniture, the carpets, the curtains—still in the fashion of the sixties, always carefully dusted, vacuumed, and polished, in the places where they have always stood.

I think about my last two sessions with Dr Goldman. Sitting there on the couch, I had begun to feel almost comfortable, as if I could talk and talk, and eventually everything would be all right.

'I'm very happy with the way things have gone,' I said. 'The headaches are much better, and I think it has been good to talk about my father.'

Dr Goldman watched me once again in silence.

'I realise that my father really failed me in a lot of ways. And I've spent so much time defending him. I just have to accept that he was a failure.'

Dr Goldman didn't reply.

'And that has helped me.' I continued. 'I was getting worked up for no reason. And I'm sure that's the reason for the headaches. So thank you. I know it's only the fifth session, but I think I'm okay now, really. The headaches are much better. There's no reason to continue.'

'There is every reason to expect that they will come back,' Dr Goldman said, 'if you don't get to the bottom of this.'

'Oh, come on!' I said, angrily. 'What do you mean? I thought this was supposed to help me.'

'How much do you really know about your father?'

'What do you mean?' I shrug. 'What is there to know? He was just an ordinary guy. He spent most of his time reading the *Sporting Globe*.'

'What about his family? His life before he married your mother? His work?'

'Well, I don't know. Anyway, I don't see why that's important.'

'At any rate, you've agreed to one more session.'

'Fine,' I say. 'I'll come, then.'

Remembering this conversation, I look around the house, feeling uncomfortable at prying into the closed world of my parents. In the corner of the room, on a shelf, I find a photograph of their engagement. My father is still in his army clothes. My mother wears a long, black dress with black gauze neck and sleeves. They both appear a little ill-at-ease with one another, as though they have just been left alone in the room for the first time. My mother's head inclines towards him slightly, and her face is uncertain. Her lips are slightly parted in a nervous half-smile. When I look closely at my father I can see the beginnings of the shrouded look which came over his face later on. I turn around with the photograph in my hand, half expecting to see him in the chair on the other side of the room. I don't know what I would expect him to say—whether he would open the locked gates of the past, with whatever feverish winds are hidden away there, or just raise his tired eyes once again with that blank look which banished me to someone else's country, someone else's life—not his.

I replace the photograph among the other objects on the shelf—a cricket trophy from the premiership we won in the last year I played; a piece of rock from Egypt; a little stand of medals: Pacific

Star, Defence Medal, A.S.M. And as I put the photograph down, I notice something bronze and slightly tarnished lying behind it. It's just a cigarette lighter but, after a moment, I recognise it as the one I gave to my father as a present when I was about sixteen. The metal lighter is enclosed by a fine network of filaments, like vines twisting around a tree. I had bought it in the same store where, as children, we had ventured on our brief career as thieves. I remember seeing it, and impulsively spending the money I'd saved for months from washing cars and other odd jobs.

'It's beautiful,' he said, when I gave it to him. 'Thanks a lot.'

'I figured it's something you could really use,' I said, gratified for once to have found some way into his affection. 'So I got it for you.'

I looked forward to seeing him flicking off the lid to light up his endless stream of Craven A cigarettes, and feeling that I had some small part in his life.

A few days later I was talking to my brother. He took out a cigarette for himself, and held out the lighter to light one for me, too. I sat there, quite still, looking at the lighter. I could feel myself turning pale.

'Where did you get that lighter?' I asked.

'Oh, I lost my other lighter, so Dad gave me this one,' Paul said. 'I guess he didn't want it.'

'He's a bloody bastard,' I said. Paul shrugged, and lit his cigarette.

'Don't get so worked up,' he said, blowing out a mouthful of smoke. 'You'll give yourself a seizure.'

Looking at the lighter again, more than thirty years later, I feel the same stab of pain and anger towards this man, with his callous silence, his emotional incapability. It was just one of the thousand tiny betrayals I felt through my childhood. What was it that made him close up so against the world, against me, and shut everything out with such doggedness, a determination he never showed in any other field of his life? I'm angry with him for fading away, for giving up and submitting to failure, for sitting day after day in the same chair, even for all the illnesses and the strokes and the hospital rooms, for walking with a limp, pulling his leg along like a dead weight. But most of all I'm angry that I was left on the sidelines for so long like a player who wasn't needed, forgotten and unwanted.

I walk out of the empty house into the garden through the sliding door, the lighter still in my hand. My knees feel a bit wobbly, and I sit down on a stump near the back door, where my father cut down a tree long ago. I feel sick, sicker than I have for a long time. I begin to remember the next part of the story I have found in Dr Goldman's office.

At twenty-one, having felt the breath of war hot on my neck and, through the quickness of my wits, outsmarted the dull bureaucrats, I felt as though my life must be enchanted, set apart from the rest. If I could not forgive my father for his failure in my need, I'd found in Max a figure who could replace him as the counsellor, supporter and confidant I wanted. I returned to my studies, which had ground to a halt under the stress of my father's constant illnesses and my sense of isolation. Life was once again something to be seized and enjoyed. My attention was divided between my car, an old Wolseley, upon which I lavished endless hours of loving care, and the hormonally tinted world of sex which opened up before me.

The girls of the early seventies, in their thigh-high boots and mini-skirts, with bandannas wrapped around cascades of hair, and flushed with new freedoms, new ideas, new pleasures were a revelation and an addiction. With each new girl I felt reborn, carried further and further from the shores of the past and its inadequacies, a yacht drifting carelessly towards the horizon. Sex thumped everywhere in the air, an addiction like the cigarettes I smoked in abundance, or the politics we talked furiously into the small hours under a haze of incense and pot smoke.

Max, too, appeared to have thrown out the sterilised caution of the fifties—he finally announced the end of the drawn-out tragedy with Susie, and moved into an apartment with Joyce. At their home, strewn with Moroccan cushions, Modigliani prints, and the free, artistic portraits Max had begun to shoot lately, I felt like a handsome bohemian prince in an open-necked shirt and shaggy hair. I had escaped at last from the grey castle of suburban unhappiness. I looked for one girl after another to confirm my metamorphosis; and more than one of them got angry—despite their advanced and libertarian ideas—at my inconstancy and restless compulsion to move on. Somehow I always needed to be the one to jump first. None of these little victories was ever quite enough.

I saw my parents less and less. I found a job that gave me my independence and took up most of my energy. I took on more and more work at the firm, hoping for recognition and advancement. I was glad not to have time to think too much about anything. If I thought about my father at all, it was only as a distant, irrelevant figure on the sidelines of my existence. A year or so later a crisis emerged in the firm, an ugly, banal tragedy of office politics which led me to leave and start out in private practice. But even then I didn't turn to my father for support or encouragement. I didn't mention it to him at all, as though to prove to myself that I never had needed and never would need anything from him.

The rooms were just bare floors and walls at first. But after a few months, one by one, my former clients moved over to my new business. I was confident once again in my talent and luck that had brought such good things out of the rubble. I hired a new secretary and, a couple of days after she started, she buzzed me on the intercom to say that a man was waiting outside. His name was Stan, she said. Could I please come out?

I walked out into the office and there he was, my father, waiting calmly on the couch, looking tired and ill as usual. I greeted him rather stiffly.

'What can I do for you, Dad?'

He looked small and old in the large, new sofa, but

unembarrassed. He suggested that we should go and get a coffee together. We walked most of the way to the cafe in silence. Then, as we turned the corner, he said that he needed to borrow some money from me.

'Just a small loan,' he said. 'I will pay it back in a month or so.'

I knew he would. He was meticulous about things like that. But I felt even further away from this man walking beside me than I had ever felt before. Somehow, his coming to me now, asking for money, made me feel hard and mean. He would not even leave me to forget about him in peace. He didn't love me or hate me— he didn't even notice me until the moment he needed money, probably for the gambling which was the only thing left that seemed to elicit any feeling from him at all. My heart tightened like a fist. I gave him the money he asked for, and left without drinking my coffee.

Walking back to the office, I thought of Max, with all his energy and enthusiasm and love. There could not be a greater contrast to the choking constriction I felt with my father. On an impulse, I walked to his apartment, but he wasn't at home. So I went to the National Gallery, where he often spent the afternoon. We could take a walk together, I thought, and look at the paintings, and the thick, oily colours would flow back into my life. I walked up and down the rooms looking for him, past the frill-collared Van Dyck portraits and the huge Tiepolo canvas of Cleopatra's banquet. I wandered through the Australian section, where Tom Roberts' shearers froze mid-snip and Streeton's streaky gum trees burst upwards toward the blazing sun.

I entered my favourite room, the modern Australian painters, and finally saw Max at the far end, in front of a grotesque biblical scene by Arthur Boyd. He was talking to two women in their late forties, gesturing a little too broadly and laughing a little too loudly. The women were dressed much younger than their age, and heavily made up. His words ran over one another in their excitement, without leaving enough time for breath. His forehead was sweating, and every time he wiped it his hair dye would smear a little onto his forehead. One of the women nudged the other with her elbow, and Max put his hand on the younger woman's arm. At that moment, he looked furtively around the room, and our eyes met briefly. He made no sign that he knew me, and looked away. Later, in the cafeteria, he rushed up and greeted me with his usual enthusiasm, expressing his surprise and joy at running into me. We talked for a while, but neither of us mentioned the little scene I had just witnessed.

A few months later I visited my parents on Sunday afternoon. My father was out in the back yard, reading the *Racing Guide*, while I helped my mother wash up. She asked me how the business was progressing. I told her things were fine. 'Well,' she said, 'your father always said you were a clever fellow.'

I stopped, and watched her scrubbing each dish with methodical care. I didn't believe her at all. I had never heard my father say anything that remotely resembled a compliment or a favourable remark. Still, I couldn't prevent an unfamiliar, warm feeling of pride from stealing over me. I said, to cover this feeling, 'Really? I didn't think he cared.'

'No, no,' my mother said. 'He just doesn't show it.'

'Why not?' I said.

'Well, you shouldn't worry,' my mother said. 'Even when Jules died, he wouldn't let anyone see him cry.' Jules was his closest friend, someone he had known all of his life in Australia. If he couldn't cry for Jules …

After a while I went out into the back yard. Dad was sitting in a red-striped folding chair, in the dappled shadow under the monsteria tree. I sat on the step. The afternoon sun shone gently on my face. After a few minutes had passed he said, 'Bernard …'

'Yes, Dad,' I answered.

'I need another loan. Just to tide me over.'

I stood up. The blood pounded like waves in my ears, and my eyes felt bruised. I stared at him, lying back in the chair, immobile. I was trembling. I wanted to shout and shout at him, shout until my voice gave out.

'No, Dad,' I said.

Noah

Now I am back in that garden once again, twenty-five years later, waiting for my mother to return. I notice that drops of rain are falling on my neck, my hair, my hands. The sky above is dark, and the drips progress quickly with the swift change of Melbourne's weather into thick, glistening drops which splash onto the faded stripes of the chairs and the table, which is dirty from lack of use. I would like this rain to fall like a deluge which would wash everything clean. I would like it to wash away the past, leaving only an ark, and Noah's dove, with the twig of olive in its beak.

That's what I tried to explain to Dr Goldman in the last session of the six weeks.

'I know that I had problems with my father,' I said. 'But there's a point where you have to leave that behind and make your own life. I tried to forget about all of that a long time ago. I met Wendy, on the first day after I moved into my new business premises, and a few months later Dad died. It was sad, I guess, but it was like a chance to start all over again. I made a decision then to think only of my future with Wendy. I would put all of the old life behind me. I left it all behind, everything that had let me down, or made me unhappy. I broke away from my family, a lot of my friends, Max—and above all, from my father. All the things that I searched for in him, all the things he failed to be, I decided to create for myself, for Wendy and the kids. I didn't need anyone else. I didn't need my father.'

'What did you feel when your father died?' Dr Goldman asked.

I am quiet for a long time. 'Nothing,' I say.

Standing at his graveside, on another soaking Melbourne day just like this, I felt nothing at all. No, that is not true. I felt an overwhelming sense of relief. The thick silence which had reigned between us would now pass at last into the permanent stillness of soil and stone—nothing could be changed any more, no-one would hope or be disappointed. And yet I was troubled by a sense of unreality. The wooden casket was much too light to hold the weight of a life. I wondered briefly if my father had simply evaporated into the air. I looked carefully at the faces of the people around me. Many of them were trembling and stained with tears. I wondered what this thing could be that touched their hearts so strangely. What could my father possibly have given them that could be repaid with such an outpouring of emotion? When it came to my account, the ledgers were empty. I felt nothing, as though I was looking down into a hollow grave. If I wished for tears, it was only to wash away the feeling of dryness that the rain could not assuage.

My brother walked forward and threw a handful of soil onto the coffin. This act of mourning would begin the Jewish ritual which surrounds and comforts those who are left behind, from the tearing of garments to the recitation of *kaddish*. But I could think only that my father had never had time for such things. He had always silently and stubbornly protested against any manifestation of religious belief, piety, or even simple observance. I remembered him reading the racing results over Urisz's prayers. I remembered his strange, unfocused look at my *barmitzvah*. And I remembered how he hadn't cried at the funeral of his friend Jules. I wondered if he would have cried at my funeral, and I thought, I just don't know. I had never understood this man who had so occupied my thoughts, and entered so deeply into my life even in his silence and his immobility. But now he was gone, and I felt relieved that it was over.

I looked around at the people standing nearby. They were all waiting for something. I was surprised by the number of people who had come to pay their last respects: business people, labourers, professionals, housewives, Jews, and Gentiles, most of them people I'd never seen. I wondered who was this man who could bring together all of these people from different corners of life, waiting there at the edge of his grave. I was waiting, too. I was standing with a handful of soil, waiting for something. But it never came. I felt something beating, far away behind my temples. I stepped back, and family members and friends made their way to the edge of the hole, and took up a handful of earth and scattered it over the wooden lid with a dull thud. One by one they filed away, and I was left standing alone in the cemetery, the wet dirt trickling through my fingers.

This is what I told Dr Goldman.

'I think that's where the headaches begin,' he said. 'Grief.'

'But I told you,' I said. 'I didn't feel anything.'

'Well, you are feeling it now. You still need to grieve.'

'But I hardly remember him any more. I never knew him properly, even when he was alive.'

'Well, that's the problem. You need to put this ghost to rest. You need to find your grief.'

A noise from inside the house returns me to the present—my mother has returned from her errand. I get up from the stump where I've been sitting, and go back into the house. My mother is walking around, putting back in place the few items that I have shifted. She looks up.

'Bernard, what are you doing? You're soaked.'

'Don't worry, Mum,' I say, smiling. 'It's okay.'

She rushes to get towels from the bathroom, wondering out loud who would be crazy enough to stand out in the rain—as though, somewhere, someone is blaming her for my being wet through. I feel almost like a child again, the ten-year-old riding my bike home from cricket practice in the rain. But now I have my own children who get wet, and muddy, and misbehave, and play cricket with an upside-down garbage bin. My mother comes back in with a towel, and I dry off. 'Here, put this on,' she says. She hands me a jacket. It is one of my father's. As I put my arms into the black woollen sleeves I feel the pull of his slighter, narrower shoulders against my own.

'Mum,' I say, 'I've been seeing a psychiatrist.'

She stares at me. There is a long silence.

'Why?' she says, looking pained. 'There's nothing wrong with you.'

'Well, for a start, there's my headaches. They just won't go away.'

'Oh, I get migraines all the time,' she says. 'I always have—surely you must remember. Always. I just take medication.'

There is a silence again. I try to focus myself.

'The doctor thinks that it's got something to do with Dad. I mean …'

I am stammering slightly. It is ridiculous. I am a grown man. I feel as though I have broken some unwritten rule. Finally I manage to say it. 'The doctor thinks I never really grieved for him when he died.'

'What do you mean?' she says, shaking her head dismissively. 'You were there at the funeral, after all. We all were. You can go to the grave any time you like.'

'But who was I burying? He never told me anything about himself.'

'What is there to say?' she says. 'He was a nice man. Ask his friends, all the family, they all liked him. Everybody liked him. He was a good man. That's all.'

'But he wasn't a good father.' I am surprised to hear myself speaking suddenly so loudly and angrily. I am surprised to hear these words coming out of my mouth at all. I feel disconnected, as though I am eavesdropping on this conversation from another room.

'You have no idea,' my mother says with an unaccustomed flash of anger in return. 'You have no idea. Your father tried his best, he always did his best for all of us. No matter what. You couldn't possibly know. You don't know.'

'No,' I say. 'I don't know. I don't know anything about him at all. Neither of you ever told me anything.'

My mother glares at me for a moment, with her mouth open as though she is about to say something. Then, after a moment, she sighs, and her anger melts away into the air. Her body seems to hunch and shrink a little.

'I've told you, there's nothing to tell,' she says, resignedly. 'Why do you need to worry about these things now? It's all over and done with a long time ago.'

As we are leaving the house, I notice that I still have the lighter in my hand. Without thinking, I go towards the shelf to put it back, and I look again at the photograph of the young couple. I observe again the shaded, withdrawn look in my father's eyes. But this time I notice that, alongside his characteristic diffidence, there is an oddly confident air, a more relaxed posture, a faint, comfortable military bearing. He is leaning back a little. His eyes are, as always, slightly hooded. For the first time I am really curious about this young man. Because this really is a young man. He is at the end of one journey and the beginning of another. I don't put the lighter back. I keep it in my pocket.

The next day I call Dr Goldman. 'I've been thinking about the last session,' I say. 'How can I grieve for someone I never really knew? I've decided to go on with this. With the therapy. And I'm going to try to find out about my father.'

Sara Marin with her daughter Gutka in August 1936

Part Two

Winter

Beeeeeeeep. Silence. Beeeeeeeep. Silence.

At midnight I try calling again. On the other end of the line, the ringing tone is now irritatingly familiar—a short, dead silence after dialling, followed by a series of disembodied clicks, and then two-second pulses of medium tone at regular intervals. In every silence I listen painfully, hoping for a voice—even the wrong one—to answer. It would comfort me to know that there is anything alive at the end of these tendrils of wire and fibre-optic cables. I feel as though the world at the other end of the line is empty, abandoned, like an episode from a 1950s science-fiction serial: a room somewhere in Israel, a telephone ringing and ringing, and then the empty streets. Silence.

So far, the quest for my father amounts to nothing but these hollow, distant tones, ringing on a continent far away. After a while it begins to sound like the bleeping of a submarine sonar, sweeping the empty sea in endless circles and finding nothing. On the table in front of me are a few meagre items, all I have managed to scavenge from the wreck of my father's life. A few pages of notes from his cardiologist, scrawled in an untidy medical hand. My father's passport. Some photographs my mother has given me of my father's family before the war: an older and a younger woman, striding along a Warsaw street; a dark-complexioned man in the middle of St Mark's Square in Venice, surrounded by pigeons; and a thin young boy with large, hooded eyes: my father. And two postcards, one from the resort of Merano in the Italian Dolomites, addressed to P. Marin, Ogrodowa 26a, Warsaw,

Poland; the other with a young boy on the front, addressed to my father's uncle, Herr J. Gerberbaum, Weimar.

When I scavenged these things from my mother I stared at them for days, looking sidelong at them while at work, leaving the dinner table with some excuse in order to look at them again. I know the names that are associated with these faces, but they mean nothing to me. Sara and Pinkus, my grandparents. Beniek and Gutka, my uncle and aunt. Looking at the photographs over and over, I feel that some of the life that was captured on that day long ago must surely spill out of the borders of the frame—the flick of a head, the creasing smile at the edge of the eyes, the look when someone is about to speak. But these moments remain inside their locked windows—still strangely alive, but trapped into the dark and shade of the monochrome photographic paper. All the same, I return to them, again and again, like a child drawn to a magic lantern. I repeat the unfamiliar names until I know their pictures by heart. Sara's sturdy frame, Gutka's shy smile, Pinkus with the pigeons taking off from his arm, his face about to break into laughter. I note the gestures, trace the lines of the faces, compare the children as they grow into adults. That way, if I had passed them on a Warsaw street, perhaps I would have been able to call to them, address them by name. But if they had turned, what would I have said then? I know nothing about them. I know only that they are dead. I cannot speak their language or share their memories. I know nothing of the strong-framed woman, the short, dark man with the moustache, the beautiful Gutka with her dark ringlets and the dashing Beniek in coat and tie. Of the little boy with the hooded eyes—my father—I know least of all. I am determined, although it is twenty years too late, to find out.

The day after the rain at my mother's house, I look through the pages of the telephone book, trying to find a Polish researcher who can help me locate any trace of the past my father has taken with him. At last I find Krystyna, a young academic. She agrees to help, and writes letter after letter to the archives in Warsaw asking for information, and places an ad in the Warsaw daily paper for several weeks.

Did You Know My Family?

I am looking for people who knew my grandparents before the war. Their names were Pinkus Marin and Sara Marin née Fogel (they were Jewish) and they lived at 26A Ogrodowa Street in Praga. I know almost nothing about them. I am researching the history of my family, almost all of whom died during the war. Pinkus and Sara had three children: Stanislaw, Beniek and Gutka. If you knew this family please write airmail.

Every day in the late afternoon I imagine that an elderly man is stumbling down to the gate of his house, his breath turning white in the cold air of the Polish morning, to find the rolled-up newspaper lying comfortably in its usual place. As he drinks his coffee, and eats thin slices of toast, his wife will look over his shoulder and say, 'Oh, goodness, the Marins—Pinkus and Sara. They had a shop next door to my parents', don't you remember?' She will search out a box full of old photographs, letters, debris from a time long past, and she will sit down and write out a long letter in a crabbed, elderly hand. Every day I wait fretfully for the letter to arrive, ringing Krystyna the minute I leave work. Sometimes her husband answers, and when he calls her from the other room I can hear the unfamiliar sounds of Polish being spoken in the background. I wait, expecting to hear that she has finally torn open the stiff white envelope which holds the key to that lost world. But when she comes to the phone she only says, 'No, I'm sorry Bernard, there's no letter.' After a while, she promises me that she will call me the moment she receives any news. I realise that my insatiable eagerness is wearing her down. It is wearing me down also.

I hear that some friends, Steven and Judy Colman, are going to Poland. I call them and ask them to try to find out anything they can while they are there. I give them a list of the questions I most need to answer. I wonder if I should be going over myself. I wait impatiently for an email. I am certain that they will have found some trace of my family. But when the email comes they tell me that it is impossible to find out much about the past—the barriers of the language and culture are too great. They tell me that they have made enquiries at a foundation in Warsaw, the Ronald S. Lauder Foundation, but all they managed to find was a telephone book from 1930 which listed Pinkus Marin, merchant. They give me the address—26a Ogrodowa Street. I go to the drawer and take out the postcard of Merano, Italy. It is postmarked 9.10.24. It is addressed to P. Marin, 26a Ogrodowa. For the first time I know the family's address for most of my father's childhood. I ask them to go to the address, if they can, and take a photo. When they arrive back in Australia they give me a single picture which they managed to take before the local residents, probably fearful of property claims, asked them to leave. I stare at the photograph and the address, excited by this discovery. But I am still no closer to penetrating the silence which separates me from these people, this apartment, my father.

After a few weeks the advertisement is pulled from the Warsaw newspaper, and I wait again. I am sure that at the last moment someone will pick up the pen and, with just a few simple scratches of ink, end the anxiety which is beginning to burn me up inside. Perhaps they have been sick, or too busy to write, but have noted down the address, and one rainy afternoon they will search out the piece of paper from the cabinet, and finally put pen to paper. My letters to the Polish archives are returned with a blank—no certificates of birth, death, or marriage exist for any of the family, not even for my father. Now the life and excitement which had burst from the precious photographs is beginning to fade, deprived of the animating force of fresh discovery. The pulsing life of these people, the immediacy of their gestures, the movements that seem almost ready to flicker back to life, all of this begins to die. I stare and stare, but I cannot recover the life I gave to these people every time I looked at them. Whenever I steal an unexpected glance once again, hoping for the return of that little flutter of excitement, all I can see is the dull, flat patterns of light and shadow. They have returned to the too-familiar faces of strangers—like faces on a train that one sees every day but does not acknowledge, as though separated by an invisible barrier. The magic lantern has stopped turning. It has left only frozen, lifeless forms, and silence. Eventually I can't bear to look at them any more, and I put them away in a drawer, inside a white envelope. Still, sometimes they haunt me at night, those photographs lying in the drawer like pressed leaves from a tree which was cut down long ago.

I go to see Dr Goldman again. I tell him that I am angry about the dead, enclosed valleys in which I have found myself. I speak for a long time. Somehow I am beginning to feel that this is some kind of punishment for trying to find out at all. I blame my father for hiding all of this away from me, and even for dying before I had the courage to ask him the questions I should have asked long ago. I am angry, too, with these people I can't remove from my head, unaccountably angry that they should die without leaving a trace, a birth certificate, a letter, anything. How can their entire existence have been erased, as though they had never lived? The doctor listens with an infuriating calm to my ranting, and then asks, 'Are you sure that nothing is left?'

'Of course,' I say. 'Otherwise I would have found something by now. The whole family just vanished into thin air. I suppose it's not all that surprising.'

'The whole family?' Dr Goldman says. He watches me steadily.

'No, not my father,' I say. 'What's the difference? He never talked about the past, and now it's too late.'

'Too late for what?' the doctor asks.

There is a silence.

'I knew this would happen,' I say. 'I knew I'd end up feeling worse than I did before. The headaches are coming back. So there hardly seems any point to it at all.'

'The headaches—are they the only reason you are doing this?' Dr Goldman asks.

'Yes,' I say. 'No. I don't know. I want it to stop.'

'It's hard to face things,' he says, 'at the cost of so much pain. Sometimes it's just too much.' I nod.

'You need to figure out why you are doing this,' he continues, 'and then perhaps you'll know whether you want to go on.'

Beeeeeeeep. Silence. The phone bleeps and bleeps, like a distant cry, repeated over and over. My letters to Poland have turned up nothing but endless referrals, and the newspaper ads have appeared and disappeared in silence. There is no old man with his trimmed beard and his white breath. There is no box full of the last traces of life, no letter full of memories, no old woman to write in a shaky hand.

'I can't believe there's nothing else,' I say to my mother. 'I just can't accept it.'

'It was a long time ago,' my mother says. 'There's nothing left except for those few photographs, and I've given them to you already. Maybe I shouldn't have. I thought they would be enough.'

'But I need to know who they were, and what happened to them,' I say. 'They are my family, after all.'

'Leave them in peace. They all died, God rest their souls. All of that—it was terrible, of course—was all over long ago.'

'That's no reason not to find out.'

'There's nothing to find out. You should be glad you don't have to live in such a horrible way. You live in a good country. Why dig up the past now? Goodness, you're nearly fifty years old!'

She stares at me in silence, with an unusual directness. She narrows her eyes slightly, as though looking at something she hasn't noticed before. For once, I have a vague sense that she has actually understood what I just said. Then she turns away, hunching her shoulders, looking tired and wounded. She seems to take my words as a reproach.

'All my life I've had this family, the Fogels, the Klepners, the Kleids, around me—Grandpa, Sabina, Nellie, Urisz, Mary and Frank, all the others. It's always been part of my life. But there have always been the shadows of the missing part, the Marins. Where are they? Who were they? But for some reason no-one ever talked about it, no-one even mentioned their names. It was as though they never really existed. But in those photographs you can see that they were really alive—so alive they could turn around and speak at any moment. But the photos aren't enough, I need to know something about them, about their lives, what happened to them.'

My mother is silent.

'Well then, I guess you win,' I say. 'I've tried, but I can't get anywhere. The Marins are all dead and gone, and that's the end of it.' But I can't help the tears welling in my eyes.

My mother doesn't reply. She gets up from her seat and goes into the other room. She is gone for a long time. I get up and call to her,

'Mum, I'm going to go now.'

'Wait,' she calls back, her voice muffled by the wall. 'Just wait for a moment.'

'No, I really have to go,' I say.

'Bernard, wait. I have something for you,' she says. After a moment she comes into the room with a piece of paper torn from a notebook.

'I really don't know if I should give you this. His name is David Sela. Your father had a cousin, Ela Marin. This is her son. Not all of the Marin side were killed in the war. Afterwards she never spoke about it, and now she has passed away, too. I met her when I went to Israel—and David, too. He still lives there with his family. He's an engineer in the shipyards in Haifa. I doubt that he can tell you anything, and I really shouldn't let you bother him. But just to satisfy you that there are some Marins left. I hope that will be enough for you.'

She looks at me as I am leaving, and I'm not sure how to read the guarded look in her eyes. Is it fear, or concern, or something else? I quickly dismiss the thought from my mind in my surge of impatience to call David Sela. The second I get out the door I try calling from my mobile. I hear the Israeli ringing tone. Beeeeeeeep. Silence. Beeeeeeeep. Silence.

And this is the sound which I have become accustomed to over the past few weeks, dialling again and again at different times the number that my mother has given me—early in the morning, late at night, making endless calculations on time zones, seasons, daylight saving. I have called the number so many times that I feel I have almost reconstructed a whole life lived in that distant land. I try to imagine their comings and goings—work, school, *shabat*, holidays—playing them out in the silences between the ringing tones, trying to second-guess the movements of people I have never met. And now it is three o'clock in the morning here, and eight o'clock in the evening there, and I am calling once again, hopelessly.

During the night I dreamed that I was in a city I did not recognise, but whose streets I somehow knew. It was a foreign city, and somehow I had arrived there without my passport or my luggage. I walked and walked, but arrived nowhere. I had an appointment in an office somewhere on the other side of the town, but as I walked faster my progress seemed to become slower and slower, until I knew I would not make it in time, and I began to panic. There was no option but to go on, but there was no longer any hope of getting there. I woke suddenly, the feeling of panic still gripping my veins, and my head throbbing. After a moment I sensed with relief that I was at home. I shook my head vigorously to dispel the last remnants of the illusion.

'Bernard?' Wendy mumbled, woken by the jolting.

'A dream,' I said. 'A bad dream. I'm going downstairs for a minute.'

I climbed quietly out of bed and went down to the kitchen. While I was getting water from the tap, almost without thinking, I grabbed the phone and dialled the number I know by heart. Now I'm listening once again to the familiar ringing. Beeeeeeep. Silence. Beeeeeeep. Silence.

Then there is a click, and a woman's voice says 'Shalom?'

I have no breath to answer.

The voice says again, 'Shalom?'

'My name is Bernard Marin,' I say. 'I'm calling from Australia. Do you speak English?'

'Yes, a little,' says the thickly accented voice.

'I would like to speak to Mr David Sela,' I say. 'I am his second cousin.'

'You are looking for David?' she asks.

'Yes, I'm his cousin, a distant cousin.'

'David is at work yet. But has mobile telephone. You wish the number?' Yes, I tell her. Yes, please. I can hardly make my hand work to write down the number, and she has to repeat it several times.

I hang up and try to dial, but I have to pause midway. I can't stop my heart from beating. The blood beating in my ears is making a hell of a noise, and I have to wait a moment before dialling again. This time I think I have the number wrong. On the third dial, I let the number click into silence and then, once again, I hear the ringing tone. After four rings a man's voice answers, and I begin to speak, but the voice continues. It is a message bank. I wait for the beep, and then leave a brief message.

'Hello, David, my name is Bernard Marin, and I am calling from Australia. My father, Stan Marin, was your mother's cousin. So we are second or third cousins. I am trying to trace our family, the Marins, and I am hoping that you can help me.' I leave all of my contact details breathlessly at the end of the message.

I stand for a few minutes in the cold kitchen, savouring the strangeness of those words 'our family'. It had never seemed real to me that somewhere out there was another branch of the tree, cut off also, and grafted in another country, another language.

Suddenly, the phone rings next to me. I pick it up.

'Hello, this is David Sela,' says the voice.

My throat is dry as I try to explain, with the slight time-delay and the breaking up of the mobile signal making the distance seem even greater.

'Yes,' he says, 'I have your message, only a few minutes. I hear it with many thanks and enjoy! Yes, I think we are related in some way, how exactly I'm not sure yet. Can you help me out in it?'

'Yes,' I say. 'You are a Marin on your mother's side, yes? Your grandfather's name was David Marin, the older brother of Pinkus, my grandfather. My mother met you and your mother Ela when she visited Israel.'

'Oh, yes,' he says. 'I think to remember. Ten years, about.'

'Can you tell me a little about yourself?' I ask.

'Yes,' he says. 'I'm fifty-two years old, born in Poland. Emigrated for Israel at the age of ten, and graduated nautical college in 1965. I have spent a lifetime from Israeli navy, most in submarine. Now retired as captain and managing industrial projects of construction. And you, what is age and occupation?'

I explain something about myself in a few sentences, racing impatiently through these formalities.

'I am trying to find out about my father's family. I don't know very much at all. If there is anything you can tell me …'

'I am sorry for this, but my mother is dead a long time ago now. In 1993 she died. Maybe she could have helped you.'

'Did she ever speak to you about her family in Poland? Perhaps she mentioned her uncle Pinkus and aunt Sara, or her cousins Beniek and Gutka and Stan?'

He thinks for a moment.

'No, I'm sorry, these names are not familiar. My mother did not like to speak of the past. It was very painful for her. Only she told us her father, David, as you said, and brothers and sisters, but not cousins.'

'And her brothers and sisters, they all died in the Holocaust also.'

'Oh, no, no,' he says. 'Only grandfather died.'

There is a silence.

'Your mother also had brothers and sisters who survived?' I ask, incredulously.

'Oh yes,' he says. 'Her sisters Sala and Guta. Also a brother. I don't remember his name. He emigrated to Argentina, before the war. We did not meet him.'

'And they are all dead now?'

'Aunt Sala, she was here in Israel, but she died two years ago. And the uncle, in Buenos Aires, he died a long time ago too. He had sons. I can find it out for you.'

'And the other aunt? She died also?'

'No, she still is living in Miami, Florida.'

I take a few moments to process this information. The phone crackles in my ear.

'She is alive?'

'Yes, certain.' he says. 'Aunt Guta. She has two sons in United States.'

'Can you tell me—what is her married name?'

He thinks for a moment.

'Is it—Kronenberg?' he says. 'No—it is Korenberg. And name of her husband is I think Szaja.'

'Do you have her telephone number?' I ask.

'I'm not sure. I will search to find it for you.'

'Yes, please. I would like to speak to her very much. She may remember something about the family in Poland.'

'Yes, it is possible. She is very old. I have not seen her since many years. I will search the number and call you again.'

He also promises to send me the answers to all my questions in a fax. I put the phone down and stand for a moment in the kitchen, feeling the cold floor against my feet. I lean on the wall, and it feels more solid against my shoulder. My stomach feels a little shaky with this new riot of information coursing through my body, like a starved man gorging himself on his first meal. When I came downstairs I was alone in the world—my brother and I were the only Marins left on the earth since the cutting down of the tree. Now, half an hour later, I have relatives on four continents, from Haifa to Buenos Aires. On the other side of the world, near the Gulf of La Plata, Marin children are running in the street calling to one another in Spanish. David's children are sitting in a schoolroom on the Mediterranean, taking their lessons in Hebrew. And Guta's grandchildren are roller-bladeing along the Miami beachfront, or drinking sodas in a gigantic mall. And my own children are asleep upstairs, in the quiet safety of a Melbourne night.

It takes an effort to climb the stairs back to bed. I am prey at last to the exhaustion which had been held off by my restless anxiety. But my head is clear for the first time in months. Even the exhaustion is welcome, as the herald of a long, deep sleep.

Spring

If I hear David's answering-machine message one more time I am sure that I will go mad. It is now a week since I spoke to him, and my frustration is mounting. He has faxed me some details on his family—dates of birth, years of death, marriages, migrations, professions. But these merely help to fill in the blanks on the family tree, the bare spaces among the spreading limbs. I am searching for the roots, for the anchoring force whose destruction has left these broken branches across four continents, including my own. And I am just one tiny piece of information away from that world, the world of Pinkus and Sara. I need the telephone number of Gita Korenberg in Miami, Florida, the last remaining member of my father's family from Poland. She is David's aunt and my father's first cousin. She is the daughter of Pinkus's older brother. I am sure that she is the key.

But that number is the one thing that David has not yet given me, for all his helpfulness. I cannot tell whether he is busy, simply can't find it, or is stalling for some reason. I can't see any possible motive for reluctance on his part, but I am surprised to find myself leaving message after message, waiting vainly for any reply. I try to search on my own while I wait, trawling the internet looking for Korenberg, or Korenburg—in desperation I try Kronenberg, Kronberg, Kronburg, all with no success. I call the operator in Miami; she listens patiently, but cannot find any listings for Korenberg. I keep trying, desperately, until after a few minutes she says, 'Sir, I'm sorry, I will have to give you a number now—do you have a name?' She gives me a Kronenberg, and I call the number, wondering what these people will think of my strange accent and slight hint of desperation. No, they've never heard of my family. 'Perhaps you know a Korenberg, Gita Korenberg?' I say, grasping at anything. They are polite, but of course they cannot help—Miami is not a village. I wonder what else I can do. After a week or so I begin to wake up during the night. I dream again about the strange, familiar city, but in this dream I have an appointment with Kronenberg, or Korenberg, and I cannot find the address. I stop people on the street, and they give me directions to follow, but after walking for a while I begin to think they have deliberately misled me. I retrace my steps, and start to run, in a panic, but then I worry that perhaps I was going in the right direction after all. I run back and forth, caught in an agony of indecision. I wake up sweating, and my legs hurt as though I have really been running through the streets.

'What happened to you last night?' Wendy says the next day. 'You know you kicked the doona right off the bed? I was frozen.'

'Sorry, I was dreaming,' I say. 'In the dream I was running.'

It happens again the next night, and the next. On the fourth night I wake up and wander through the house. When I come back into the bedroom, Wendy is awake, sitting up in the bed. She looks at me with tired eyes, but I can see that she has been thinking and has come to a decision.

'Bernard,' she says, 'you've got to do something about this. It's really getting out of hand. It can't go on this way.'

'I know,' I say. 'It's incredibly frustrating.'

'No,' she says, 'not that. You really are becoming obsessive about your family history. I worry about you. I think you need to let it rest for a while.'

'That's ridiculous. I've left it far too late already. If it doesn't happen soon it might not happen at all.'

'But you haven't worried about it for the last fifty years. So what difference does a few days make? You need to get some sleep, for goodness' sake. And so do I.'

'Well, I don't expect you to understand,' I say. 'You knew

your parents perfectly well. You had an ideal relationship. But Dr Goldman said that I haven't grieved for my father. And that's the reason for my headaches. So I have to find out something about him, and then maybe I can let it go.' I am pacing the floor.

'Bernard, calm down.' Wendy says. 'Honestly, do you really think this is the way to go about it? Can't you just ask your mother? She must know quite a lot—after all, living with him for forty years …'

'Come on!' I interrupt her mid-sentence. 'You know my mother perfectly well. She won't tell me anything I don't drag out of her. It's like getting blood from a stone.'

'Look, why don't we go away for a couple of weeks? We're just about due for our annual holiday with Judy and Maurice.'

'I couldn't possibly. Not now. I just have to find this one phone number. It's driving me mad.'

Wendy shakes her head despairingly and lies down in the bed. She reaches over to switch off the light.

'I'm sure it would be easier to just ask your mother,' she says, flatly.

I see Dr Goldman again, and explain about the dreams, and the night waking and the argument.

He listens and says, 'It's all part of the healing process. You have to take things as they come. Perhaps it's a good idea to get away for a while. It will give you some time out. You shouldn't push yourself so hard. You can't expect everything to turn up on order.'

But I do expect it to turn up, and turn up quickly. I won't stop now. I am convinced that if I phone one more time, if I do one more search on the internet, or post one more ad, I will discover the information that I need.

A few days later I arrive home from shopping, both hands laden with bulging white plastic bags when, through the door, I hear a message being recorded onto the answering machine. I fumble with the keys, but by the time I get through the door the caller has hung up and the machine is beeping aimlessly. When I play back the message I find that it is from David Sela. He says nothing, only that he is sorry to have missed me and will call back again. I am furious to have missed speaking to him by so little, and I call him back immediately. But once again I hear a click and go to his message bank. I slam down the phone, and look back at the litter of cans and plastic and cardboard boxes I have dropped in my dash for the phone. Apples have rolled under the couch, and a cornflakes box is leaking slowly onto the floor. I am surprised at this—surprised by this indication that my life seems somehow to have fallen out of gear, upsetting its unassailable middle-class routine, its comforting safety and predictability. An orange mournfully descends the stairs, one by one. And all of this because of one phone number, I think.

After a minute or so, Wendy walks in to find me retrieving the groceries from their retreats and hiding-places. She looks at me, about to say something, but I say, 'About that holiday. What do you think about Noosa? Just to relax for a couple of weeks, nothing else. Mum can look after the kids.'

'You've missed a capsicum,' she says. 'There, under the sofa. Noosa's a great idea. Couldn't be more perfect!'

It's a couple of weeks before we can get away. On the first day in Noosa, watching the sea driving against the coast, I wonder as usual about time passing, and think anxiously about all the things I have to do at home, at work, with the kids. But then I remind myself that I have paid for this holiday in order to unwind this stress, and I try to force my mind to go blank. I try to empty the sea of its associations. I try to forget the photographs and the postcards, the little man with pigeons on his arm, the small boy with the hooded eyes, the sounds of a strange language. I try to forget Warsaw, Berlin, Haifa, Buenos Aires, Miami. I try to forget all of the other continents that these waves wash against as they roll back from this calm, bright shore of white sand and slow-waving palms. I begin to feel that life is easy and well planned once again. Things are as they should be.

After a week or so it occurs to me that I have forgotten that number that was drumming an endless tattoo through my head. Was it a three or a four? No, it was three-four-three-eight. Or four-three-four-eight? No, I can't remember it after all. I am relieved to be a little free from that beating obsession. A couple of days go by without my calling home to check the messages twice a day. On the way out of the hotel I don't bother stopping to check my email. I begin to wonder how I have allowed things to get so out of alignment. I would never tolerate such disorder at work. I think with satisfaction of the orderly parade of clients, accountants, and secretaries in and out of my office. When something needs to be done it is done quickly, without messiness or fuss; everything is reason and control. This is how things are meant to be. I look at the calm faces of the holiday makers strolling through the shops, taking a break from their stressful working lives, just like me. There is no reason why any of the things I am trying to find out about my father should not be undertaken in the same controlled, calm, unruffled manner. When I watch the waves beating against the shore they are only waves again, after all.

Wendy looks calmer, too—she can see me taking a greater interest again in the everyday concerns of our lives—the house, the garden, the kids and their future. On the plane trip back to Melbourne she falls asleep on my shoulder, and I watch the clouds from the window, proud of my effort of control. A sense of proportion is all that is needed. The sun reflects dazzlingly from the wing of the plane as it tilts into its descent, and I wince a little as the jagged brightness flashes into my eyes. But it is only the sunshine, and soon we are driving along the freeway, past familiar landmarks, with the drowsy familiarity of a journey that we have made so many times before. There are no strange cities, no frightening dreams. There is only this sun-drenched landscape of asphalt and eucalyptus, the signs marking the suburbs, and the gardens full of tall trees and camellias turning brown in the sun.

Back into the routine of daily life, I begin the search again, more calmly and systematically. I leave one message for David Sela, telling him I have returned from my trip. But I do not call him again. Krystyna begins to work on tracing the fate of my father's relatives after he left Poland. She writes to the Holocaust Museums and Archives in Poland, Yad Vashem in Israel, the Shoah Foundation in the USA, asking for any record of their names. I contact the Miami Hall of Records, and place an ad in the *Miami Jewish Herald* looking for the Korenbergs. On the internet I find a book listing the names of the inhabitants of the Vilna ghetto, where my father's brother and sister may have fled. Then we wait for a reply from Yad Vashem, and for the book to arrive from Lithuania. I am happy to be progressing forward calmly, with no trace of the disorganised rush which had beset me before I went away. I patiently file away all the information I have collected in a folder, and I am pleased with my progress.

I try also to contact the family in Buenos Aires. I write several letters without any reply. Finally, I receive an email from a friend of the family who works at the Jewish Genealogical Association in Argentina. He informs me that he has read my letters and translated them for my cousins Eva Szelubski and Sam Marin. He regrets that their father died in an accident in 1957. They are happy to know of my existence, but they cannot tell me much about the family history. I write again, hoping for some information, or the telephone number of Gita in Miami. One day I receive a call from Sam's daughter Banina. She has difficulties speaking English, but she manages to let me know that they do not have the contact details for any of the family in Miami. It is far away, and a different language. It seems that we are destined to remain marooned on our different continents, divided by distance and culture.

A couple of weeks after my return I have lunch with a solicitor, a friend I have known for many years. We talk about the legal profession, which I know well through my brother, and the endless accumulated details of the business world in which I am immersed. It is reassuring, sitting in the RACV club, drinking the

Giesen Sauvignon Blanc, and falling into the easy ebb and flow of conversation with an old friend. We have sat here many times before, at the same table where Andrew has sat for the last twenty years, every day at lunchtime. What a model of persistence, I think. It flits into my mind momentarily how thoroughly things have returned to normal.

'I haven't seen much of you recently!' Andrew says. 'You should come and work out with me at the gym. You're really getting out of shape.'

'Next week,' I say. 'Definitely. Actually, I've had my mind on other things over the past few months.' I begin to tell him the story, and I find myself talking for a long time. He is listening intently.

When I finish, he says, 'Bernard, I've got a client who's going to Miami this week.' I look at him blankly.

'He's also a friend. I'm sure he wouldn't mind doing a little sleuthing for you.'

I manage to collect myself.

'That would be great. Anything would be a help.'

'Sure. Just write down what you want to know, and I'll give it to him.' I give him a piece of paper with 'Korenberg' written on it. 'Korenberg, Gita. Son—Marcus Korenberg.' And all my contact numbers.

I leave the restaurant feeling a little shaky once again.

A few days later, at work, my secretary buzzes me.

'Bernard,' my secretary says, 'there's a call from Miami.'

She puts the call through.

'Hello, is that Bernard?' the voice says. 'This is Andrew's friend, Peter. I'm in Miami, and I think I've found what you're looking for. Only it's not Korenberg. It's Kornberg. Marcus Kornberg. There's a number, if you want it.'

'Okay, go ahead.' I say, and take down the number. 'What's the time there now?'

'It's five o'clock. What's the time there, about nine?'

'Yes,' I say. 'Just starting off the day. Thank you. It's a big help.'

'Sure,' he says. 'No problem.'

When I've hung up, I stare at the piece of paper for a moment. It seems strange after all the wasted effort that it should come so easily. I feel quite calm.

I dial, and the phone rings at the other end. It rings and rings, and no-one answers. But I am not upset—I am sure that things will work out in a good, orderly way, without panic or messiness. I work steadily through the morning and then, around lunchtime, I try calling again. This time a voice answers, a woman's voice with a strong Floridean accent.

'Hi, this is Marlene Kornberg,' she says.

'Marlene,' I say, 'my name is Bernard Marin. I'm calling from Melbourne, Australia. Are you a relative of Gita Kornberg? If so, I am your second or third cousin.'

'Yes,' she says. 'I think you want to speak to my husband, Marcus.'

'I'm very glad to have found your number at last—it took me quite some time. David Sela in Israel gave me your name, but he didn't have your number. But things have their way of working themselves out.'

'I'm sorry,' she says, 'but my husband is out. Can you call back in an hour?'

The hour drags past, but finally I dial again. Marcus answers.

'So you're a cousin?' Marcus says, excitedly. 'In Australia? Wow, that's quite a surprise!'

'I'm doing a family history, and I need some help.'

'Sure,' he says. 'Anything I can do.'

'Well, it's your mother I was really hoping to speak to. She's the only one left in my father's family, the only one who knew him before the war. I'd be so grateful if she could spare me some time.'

There is a silence. After a moment he speaks, quietly.

'I'm sorry,' he says. 'That's not possible. My mother passed away a few weeks ago.'

A few weeks ago—while I was in Noosa, watching the waves recede from the shore. I am angry with myself, so angry that for a moment I forget that he is still on the other end of the line.

After a long silence I say, 'I'm very sorry to hear that.' My voice sounds funny, as though it is echoing off the walls.

'Did she leave anything behind?' I ask, trying to remove the rising tone of desperation from my voice. 'A diary, letters, anything she had written?'

'No,' he says. 'Sorry.'

'There has to be something.'

'Well, of course, there were a few bits and pieces,' he says. 'She asked us to destroy most of it, and we did. So we have a couple of photographs, and that's all, really.'

I thank him and hang up the phone. Then I call him back straight away. When he answers, he sounds a little strained.

'If there's anything left, anything at all, can you send it to me?' I say.

'There really isn't anything you could use.'

'Anything, please. You see, she was the only one left of my father's family before the war.'

'I'm sorry to hear that,' he says, 'but there's really nothing left. She's gone. I'm sorry.' He hangs up the phone.

I stare around the office, and I am angry at my idiotic belief in the order of things. It is as though an invisible wind has blown through the papers and the filing cabinets and the pot-plants and the wood panelling, sending everything slightly off-balance. Even the floor no longer feels solid under my feet, as though the waves are pulling down from below, lurching the deck of the ship alarmingly. I feel nauseous.

'I don't really see why you're so upset,' Paul says. 'After all, you never even met her.'

He has come over at Wendy's behest. She is worried.

'I've told you, Dr Goldman says I haven't grieved for Dad. That's why.'

'What do you mean?' Paul says. 'You were at the funeral.

Anyway, I can't see what that has to do with this woman in Miami.'

He seems a little irritated, but as usual he disguises it with a relaxed, poised manner, leaning back in the chair, his arms behind his head, one leg crossed casually over the other.

'You don't understand,' I say. 'I've been searching for her for months. She was the only one left who could tell me about Dad.'

'But she can hardly have known him—maybe when he was a little kid, that's all.'

'That's what I need to know. What happened to his family. I think it's important.'

'Well, we know that. They all died in the war. Max must have told you that, surely.'

'Yes, but how did they die?'

'I don't know. He just told me they were in the ghetto or something. Maybe they were in a camp. At any rate, I guess Dad couldn't find out anything after the war. Or maybe he didn't want to. I can't see why you get so worked up about it.'

I stare at him. He looks quite calm.

'I don't understand,' I say. 'Haven't you wondered who they were, how they lived, what happened to them? Our grandparents, our uncle and aunt?'

There is a long silence. Paul is looking at me.

'No,' he says, finally, reluctantly. 'I guess I haven't.'

It is strange, but I have the feeling that he has never registered this odd fact before. He looks annoyed.

'Well,' he says. 'I don't see that there's much point in it, anyway. It was a long time ago.'

'Yes,' I say. 'Maybe you're right. Why bother trying to find out about Dad. God knows I've tried. I'm just wasting my time. He was determined to take it all with him. Now this woman is dead, and she was the last of his family. So it's finished.'

'Well, not really,' Paul says.

'What do you mean?' I say. 'Believe me, I've searched all over the world. Dad's father only had two brothers we know of, and they're both dead, and so are all their children. Gita Kornberg was the last one.'

'So what about Nellie?'

I shake my head. It's very irritating that Paul always thinks he knows better.

'What about her?' I say. 'She's Mum's cousin.'

'No, she was Dad's cousin, too.' Paul says. 'You know Mum and Dad were first cousins. So the family is all jumbled up together.'

He's right. I never thought about it properly.

'Actually Nellie and Dad were pretty close. I remember Max saying that Nellie used to live with Dad's family for a while, before the war. But I'm sure you know that already.'

I stare at him in silence for a little while.

'You mean she lived with Pinkus and Sara in Warsaw?'

'Well, yes. I guess so. That's what Max told me. Look, maybe I've got it wrong, but I'm pretty sure that's the story.'

'How long did she live there?'

'I don't know anything else. You should just go see her. She's at the Montefiore Homes for the Aged.'

'Yes,' I say. 'I know. Actually I've been to see her a few times, with the kids. I can't believe I didn't think about that. I'll go and see her first thing tomorrow.'

Paul shrugs, and says 'Well, I've got to be going now. Things to do.'

That night I don't sleep well. I am counting the hours on the clock, waking repeatedly until morning finally arrives. I get out of bed and look at the family tree I have drawn, with its spreading branches. I have looked at it so many times, trying to piece together the fragments of information, slowly filling in the bare patches with what I have learned from David Sela and Marcus Kornberg. But I have missed the other tree which spreads and interlaces its branches among this one—the tree of my mother's family, who are another outgrowth from the same roots, the same soil. Now I feel at last that I might be able to dig down into this soil to discover where my father came from, where I came from. I go back to bed and sleep fitfully for a few hours. On the way to Montefiore in the car I feel tired but clear-headed, free of the headaches for the first time in months. When I walk through the glass doors of the home I wonder what this world might be that is about to open up before me.

The River

The afternoon sunlight falls through the window of Nellie's room at Montefiore, giving a faint glow to everything. The high, quavering voice of the elderly lady sitting in a cane chair seems to drift from a lost city thousands of miles away, but separated by more than distance or time. Outside, the streets of Melbourne seem filled with a clamour of ghosts: fashionably dressed women pushing prams through the Saski Gardens, a young man in a long black coat and peaked cap carrying tied-up parcels home along Niska Street, a crowd gathering excitedly around a speaker in Krasinski Square. After some prodding, Nellie, my father's cousin, begins to tell me about my father's family, the first time I have heard anything more than vague, shadowy names: Pinkus, Sara, Beniek, Gutka. This was Nellie's world, too, for a time.

26a Ogrodowa Street. The Marin apartment was filled with the accumulated belongings of an upper middle-class Warsaw family: expensive sofas covered with chintz and draped with fringed antimacassars; glinting crystal and patterned china in dark mahogany cabinets; stiff, immaculate white sheets in the linen press; and a row of cream meerschaum pipes on the wall. But it was filled also with distant sounds which floated through open windows from the courtyard below. Up the hill from the river floated the sounds of the city: the trams clanking along the wide boulevards; the faint clatter of carts across the great paved square of Rynek Starego Miasta, overlooked on all sides by high gabled shopfronts; the confusion of bells clanging from steeples and cupolas. From the back streets came the sounds of the Jewish part of the city, which still carried here, on its furthest edge: the low murmur of the *cheder* where small, dark-capped children learned Hebrew on long tables lined with books; the hollow rattle as peddlers and traders pushed their wheeled carts down irregular flights of steps and through low-arched alleys; and a distant symphony of whirrs, bangs, and thuds from sewing-machines in garrets, cobblers in basement workshops, and scarved housewives beating carpets on window sills. This is where I begin my quest: at the boundary between these two overlapping worlds, in an avenue lined with trees and small courtyards, near the corner where the trams turned squealing into the Jewish quarter.

'I am surprised you didn't come to see me before,' Nellie says. 'And now I'm much too sick to tell stories. Not that there is anything to tell. Why would you be interested? Such a long time ago. Your father was just a little child. Little Stasiek.'

'Stasiek?' I had heard the family use this name before, but all of his friends and colleagues called him Stan.

'Yes, yes, your father. Little Stasiek. He was just like a little brother to me. I was so sad to leave him behind,' she says. 'Of course, his full name was Stanislaw—it wasn't a Jewish name. It was the name of a Polish king, I think. His brother and sister had Yiddish names, Beniek and Gutka, but Stasiek was the youngest, born after the war ended. And when the news came that we weren't part of Russia anymore, that Poland would be independent, Pinkus, your grandfather—and I remember like it was yesterday how he opened up his safe, and gave piles and piles of worthless Russian money to me and Ben to play with, and we pasted so many thousands of roubles onto leftover cardboard bolts from rolls of cloth in the warehouse—Pinkus was happy to be now Polish in the new republic. He said, 'I will call my son a Polish name. A new name for a new beginning.'

'My mother wouldn't listen to him. "This is not our country," she said. "We must all leave here, go to another place where life is not so dangerous." She was always frightened, you see, because my father had to run away from Poland. He had deserted from the Polish army in 1915. So he couldn't ever come back to live in Poland. My parents went to Germany, and I stayed behind in Ogrodowa Street, with Pinkus, and Sara—my mother's sister—and Beniek and Gutka and Stasiek. But soon Germany was not safe, either.'

Nellie pauses for a while. She gazes out of the window, as though looking for something.

'When the time came for me to leave Warsaw,' she says, 'it was a terrible parting. Yes, I can understand what Stasiek felt when he had to leave, too. What a funny little child he was. He was only about seven or eight when I left. When I said goodbye, although I was almost his sister, everyone was crying, but not him. He stood there for a little bit, looking surprised, and then he asked me if he could have my old perfume bottles. He said, "They will be very useful to me." I asked him if he was sorry to see me go away, and he thought for a while, very seriously, then he nodded. I was very pleased. Then he said, "But Mummy says I can have your wardrobe."' Nellie laughs—an old lady's wheezy, breathless laugh.

'Even Felicia, the little French governess, was crying a little, and dabbing at her eyes with her scented handkerchief.' Nellie laughs again, arching a black-pencilled eyebrow.

'But then I'm sure that was for Beniek's benefit. He was fifteen like me, and so very handsome and clever. She was rather thin. But she was devoted to little Gutka—oh, Gutka was so pretty and well-behaved. Me, she liked not so much, being an extra addition to the family. Not quite entitled, I think she felt. Later I heard a rumour that certain nights, when the maid who shared her room was away—for her night off, maybe, or gone with Sara on a shopping trip—Felicia would invite Beniek into her bed to share ... well, you know what I mean.' Nellie pauses for effect. 'But I'm sure it isn't true. No,' she says resolutely, 'I never was one to gossip.'

'But he really was quite an adventurous young fellow all the same,' she continues. 'Always joking and teasing. He would tell me that my father would fall off into the sky in Australia, because he would be upside-down. And he would ask little Stasiek to lend him money to build a crystal radio set, and Stasiek gave him all his pocket money. He would talk about this radio, all the things they would do, how they would listen to London and Paris, and he would describe all the wonderful programs that they would hear: the bands playing beautiful waltzes, and the comedies, and the football games played in Cracow and Vilno. And he would keep adding new improvements, and inventing more wonderful stories, and borrowing more money. But, of course, there was no radio at all. And this went on for months until one day Stasiek realised how he was being tricked, and he wept and wept. But, really, I think Beniek enjoyed making up the whole thing much more than he wanted the money.'

'Pinkus gave Stasiek all the money back. He was very kind, and hated to see anyone upset. Sara, on the other hand, didn't approve of tears or high spirits and fanciful ideas. She and my mother, and also your mother's father, Nathan, came from a very religious family, the Fogels—oh, very much so, like my husband, bless his soul. My grandfather Ephraim Fogel would go to *shule* every day in his old black coat down to his knees, and only walk to synagogue at Sabbath, and he would bring the poor Jews home for a meal. And his wife Dvoira kept a real kosher household, always wore a black *sheitel* on her head. Sara wasn't religious, herself, especially being married to Pinkus, and with her love of the high life on the Nalewkis, dinner parties and trips to the theatre, but still she was sometimes a little bit severe—she wasn't one to show her feelings.'

I think of my father, and the blank looks that he would sometimes have, as though some sense of affection was missing, and I wondered if he saw the same expression pass now and then across his mother's face. Nellie has stopped speaking.

'One day I had a letter from my father, and it simply said, "Nellie, we are to go to Australia. America doesn't want us." I looked on the globe in uncle Pinkus's study, and saw this great blue space between tiny Poland and the big island all the way around on the other side. I stared and stared, until it made my dizzy. My uncle came in and found me fainted near the desk. He took me in his arms and begged me to stay with them in Warsaw. He said, "It's as if I am losing my daughter." But my aunt Sara came in and said, "Don't be so silly, Pinkus, she must go with her family." Then she said, in a low voice to him, "Anyway, we have enough troubles for ourselves. You should think of that." Pinkus said, "How can we let her go? She's no more than a child." But Sara said, angrily, "She's fifteen, and it's time for her to make her own way in the world. She will be better off in Australia. Try to be sensible."

'Of course, it's true that Pinkus was a gambler, and they say that he lost a lot of money that way. He loved the excitement of cards, smoke filling the room, and the shouting, and the silence when the stakes were high. And the racing track, too, with the men in rich fur-collared overcoats and the women in beautiful dresses and big hats, and the rush to the betting windows before the race, and the hush as the horses left the blocks. But to me he was not a gambler, just a warm and generous uncle. Sometimes Gutka and I would go with him to his big warehouse on Gesia Street, and he would let us choose what we liked from the most beautiful fabrics from France or Italy to have a new dress made for the season. And sometimes, also, I would go with him to collect the rents at an apartment block he owned in 16 Mila Street in Warsaw. Every week he would set up a table in the courtyard so the tenants could pay their rent. And those who couldn't pay, he would just wave his hand and say, "What's a week or two, after all?"

'And he was always buying new things for his wife, too—on top of all the things she bought for herself—like crystal vases and silver candlesticks and the most beautiful astrakhan coat. I will always remember her in that coat—it was deep brown like autumn leaves and edged with soft grey fur. I remember that, just after she bought it, Pinkus's younger brother, Julian—he always had a reputation as a playboy, but finally he married a rich French girl called Ruth—came to visit Warsaw on his honeymoon, and we all went together to the opera in a *dorozka*– a horse-drawn carriage.'

I think of my father sitting in his chair, in the corner of the lounge, reading the *Sporting Globe*, and I wonder if he was troubled by these memories of the wind ruffling his hair in the open carriage, his mother in her astrakhan coat, carrying piles of parcels from the fashionable Warsaw stores, Beniek laughing and flirting with the young French girl, and weaving marvellous stories about the crystal radio set.

'On the day when my mother came to take me away from Warsaw, I could hardly believe I would leave this world behind me, the Roman theatre in the Lazienki Gardens, sitting in the big Tlomackie Synagogue at Pesach, shopping on Nalewki in the rush of people coming in and out of revolving doors, and talk and excitement everywhere. And it was strange, too, to know that I would not see my second family for many years, if ever again. They came to the station to see us off.

'Beniek, who was the same age as me, was happy—he said, "I will go to Australia, too, and make my fortune." He talked and talked about the things he could do in Australia, with his friends, how they would have a great farm and sheep and cattle, and ride around on horses all day. It made me a little happier to get onto the train, just when my heart was beginning to sink. And Pinkus was so upset, he wouldn't speak, and little Gutka wept floods of tears. But Sara stood there very calm, and said, "It will be better for you in Australia. Never look back." She had made us a little parcel of food for the train—she was a very good cook—but never a tear would you see from her eyes.

'Only once did I see her overcome with emotion,' Nellie says, after a moment. 'Not long before I left Warsaw. We were at the Summer Theatre in the Saski Gardens where every year they held the Paderewski Piano Competition. In every school in Warsaw, piano students tried to be selected for the competition, where they would play alongside the most talented pianists in Europe. And of all these, Beniek, your uncle, was chosen to compete. When he walked on stage he was shining with joy. And when I turned I saw the same look on his mother's face, as though she had overcome all her stiffness. He played so beautifully, and while he was playing … it's silly … but it seemed as if everything would work out all right.'

The tired look has gone from Nellie's face. The look in her eyes must be the same look that she had as she listened to Beniek play. I imagine the family—Pinkus, Sara, Gutka, my father, and their friends and family from all over Warsaw, in the great hall with the stage and the grand piano. And I can almost hear the river of sound flowing over them like the great Vistula itself, like the sun on the lake in the Saski Gardens, like the tide of people swelling in and out of the Jewish quarter, through the market and along Okopowa Street, past the ancient synagogue and the Jewish cemetery, and out into Warsaw and beyond: to Cracow, Marienbad, Minsk, Belgrade, Prague, Berlin. It was a great swelling river of music and commerce, of language, faith, life.

'But I was wrong,' Nellie says. 'And I never saw any of them again. Only your father was left of the whole family.'

She stops. The look slowly fades from her eyes.

'What happened to them?'

'I'm tired now,' she says, turning her head away. 'I'm an old lady.'

'I have so many questions.' I say. 'Can I come again in a week?'

'You're a fool to waste your time worrying about such things, Bernard. You can see I have nothing at all to tell.'

'Well,' I say, my heart dropping, 'I won't come again, if you're too sick.'

'Do as you please,' she says, and sighs. 'It's too much, I suppose, to expect any peace until I'm dead.'

All week I wait impatiently to speak to Nellie again. I hope that the next part of her story might shed some light on the fate of my father's family. I think of everything I have read about the Holocaust. I am sure that it must be possible to discover what happened to these people caught in the whirlwind of this history. I think of Sara and Pinkus, with their arguments over gambling and expensive china. I think of Beniek going to university, and practising on the piano for hours every day. I think of Gutka, walking to school with her friends, perhaps meeting a young man in the gardens, going to see a black-and-white film in the cinema. I find a map of Warsaw, and trace the journeys they might have made, plotting out the synagogue, the warehouse, the flat on Ogrodowa, the tram. I can hardly bear to lose this beautiful world, but I know it must come to an end—the end of this world, the end of my father's family. For the first time, I begin to understand what this 'Holocaust' means. I feel the flames licking at the edge of this world, and I wait with mounting impatience to see Nellie again.

When I arrive at Montefiore I go to Nellie's room. It is empty. I stand in the middle of the room, and my stomach turns at the possibility. It can't be so. I would have heard. I stride back to the lobby. The young girl at the desk is talking in Russian on the phone.

'Excuse me,' I say. 'Where is Nellie Goldberg?' She puts her hand over the receiver.

'Can't you wait a moment?' she drawls.

'Now look,' I say angrily, 'she is a relative of mine. It's very important. Now can you tell me where she is?' I demand, angrily.

'Goldberg.' she says, calmly. 'I find out for you.' She goes into the office for what seems like an age. I drum my fingers on the desk nervously. Finally she comes back.

'She was sick yesterday. She had to go to hospital.'

'Which hospital?' I ask.

'I think Alfred Hospital.'

'You think or you know?'

'I check for you,' she says.

'No, don't bother,' I say. I call the Alfred on my mobile. She is there. I ask to speak to her.

'Hello?' she says.

'Nellie, Bernard.' I say. 'Can I come and talk to you.'

'I'm dying, and you want me to tell stories,' she says, and hangs up. I stand in the street outside Montefiore, and I wonder what to do now. After a while I begin to feel terrible about Nellie.

The next day I take her some flowers in the hospital. She is looking better. I ask the doctor how she is going. He says that she's recovering well, but she needs to rest. In spite of myself, I can't help asking how long. He looks a bit askance at my question. Four to six weeks, he says. She should be all right by then.

Four to six weeks. I can hardly contain my disappointment. I feel as though I am caught, along with the Marin family of Warsaw, in an agony of waiting and not knowing. But, unlike them, I know what the end will be. I just don't know how.

To keep my mind off the waiting I decide to look into my father's life in Australia, and his wartime service. I go to my mother's, and ask her what she can give me.

Joining Up

My mother is looking through boxes, murmuring at the growing disorder her efforts are creating. At the bottom of a box she finds a pile of letters, and flicks through them. They are old, some typewritten, others in spidery handwriting. 'Here,' she says. 'I don't know what on earth you want these old things for, but you're welcome to them.'

They are written in a language I can't read, with crossed 'l's and tiny loops, dots, and strokes over the otherwise familiar letters. 'They're in Polish anyway,' my mother says. 'So I can't see that they're much use to anyone.'

At the top of the first letter is the imprint of a stamp:

ARTICLES TRICOT ET BONNETERIE

'BOTRICOT'

25, Rue Au Maire, Paris 3e

Tel. ARC. 15-28

The date, too, can be read: 4 Decembre, 1956.

'I can get them translated,' I say.

My mother looks them over again, shrugs, and hands them over.

'I'm trying to find out something about Dad.'

'What is there to find out?' my mother says, throwing objects back into the wooden boxes.

'For a start, how he ended up in Australia.'

'Well,' says my mother, 'you hardly need to have me digging through boxes for that. I can tell you.'

'Really?' I ask, a little suspiciously.

'Yes, of course. Don't you know that Mum and I lived with your father's parents when I was very small? It was just after Nellie and her mother left to come here. Sara was my aunt—my father's sister. We stayed there for two years. Then we left, too, and came to my father in Australia.'

'So you remembered Dad from Poland?'

'No, I was only three or four. But, actually, I do remember that he wouldn't let me near the family piano.' She laughs, despite herself. 'I always wanted to sit on the stool and bang on the keys like Beniek.'

'But why did you leave Poland?' I ask.

'My father came to Australia because of Leah, his eldest sister—he was devoted to her. When Jacob and Leah went to Germany, leaving Nellie in Warsaw, he went with them. That's where he met my mother. And when they came to Australia, he came out, too, and then brought us out after him. It was a terrible journey, six weeks of rough seas and inedible food, and we had to share one cramped cabin with another family. I had my fifth birthday on the boat. Mum made a little party of mushroom soup and some cake she managed to find for me. It was so strange. I remember arriving on the wharf in Port Melbourne. There was this man standing there. He was holding a great big kewpie doll with bright blue eyes. He was my father. But I didn't know who he was, because I hadn't seen him for years.'

'And what about Dad? Did Grandpa send for him, too?'

'No, not exactly.' She pauses for a moment. 'Jacob, Nellie's father, was the one who sponsored him.'

'And what was he like when he arrived?'

'There was a crowd of us at the wharf, my parents, and Leah and Jacob and Mary. We were really excited, especially Mary and me. The ship seemed to take forever to pull in—and then the crowds of people, pushing and rushing to find their relatives, you know how people are. And we waited and waited, and we were calling out, 'Stasiek, Stasiek,' but there was no sign of him at all. We started to wonder if something had changed at the last minute, and if the letter hadn't reached us in time. But then, as the last passengers picked up their suitcases and bags and walked away, we saw a boy leaning against a post, smoking a cigarette, with just one suitcase in the other hand. He looked sophisticated and grown-up, as if he had already seen a lot of things, and come a long way. And I suppose he had.' My mother recollects herself. 'I suppose you want the passport, too, Bernard?' she says, sighing audibly.

'Yes, definitely.'

She hands me a few papers from my father's military service, some medals, and my father's passport, marked SERI NR 705903 RZECZPOSPOLITA POLSKA, and starts to put the rest of the things back in the box. She picks some letters, and flicks through them.

'Here,' she says. 'You might as well have these, too. They're just old letters from someone, but take them, anyway.'

I look over her shoulder at the small pile of yellowing sheets. I can't read the language.

'They're in Polish,' my mother says. 'So they probably won't be any use to you.'

'I can get them translated,' I say.

That afternoon I begin with my father's passport, marked SERI NR 705903 RZECZPOSPOLITA POLSKA. Inside is the stamp of the *Inspektor Emigracyjny* 3525/37, then the transit stamp from Le Havre, France, 21 April 1937, and the embarkation stamp at Toulon, 30 April 1937. Finally, there is a visa issued by the British Passport Office in Warsaw, No 87066, issued 7 April 1937, with consular stamps totalling one pound, six shillings and sixpence, and above it, MARIN—Stanislaw, Landing Permit No 12353, valid until 7 December 1937, dated Canberra, Dep. of the Interior, 7/12/36.

All that is left of my father's journey from Poland is these few frankings from official stamps. It is strange that these spidery patterns of ink on a page can carry a boy from one side of the world to another, and stand as the barrier between death and life. I try to follow his journey. He must have left from a Baltic port in Poland, probably Gdynia, for Le Havre. Then followed the long overland journey to the other side of France, to Toulon, on the Mediterranean. Then out into the sea off the Bay of Lion, steaming past Corsica, Sardinia, Malta, Crete, and down through the Suez Canal, passing through narrow passages between rock walls, and along wide shallow banks covered with dunes, and the occasional small oases of irrigated farms. Then the ship travelled out into the Red Sea, past Aden, and across the Arabian Sea to Bombay and Ceylon, still part of the British Empire.

I imagine him, a sixteen-year-old, watching all these places and peoples flying past him, walking up and down the crowded deck, staring at dolphins and flying fish from the rail. As the climate changes from the northern spring to the tropical heat, he wipes sweat from his brow, drinks gallons of water, and plays cards below deck in the evening. And on 25 May the *Oronsay* steams through the heads into Port Phillip Bay. I wonder what he feels when he sees this throng of uncles, aunts, and cousins on the Melbourne pier, and realises at last that he has left his country and his family behind. I ask my mother when I see her.

'So, what did you think of him?' I ask.

'Oh, I don't know, Bernard,' she says. 'Why are you always asking questions?' She waves me away, and continues with her nervous cleaning, which never seems to end.

In desperation, I hire another researcher to find out what she can about my father's war service. She contacts the archives, and advertises in the veterans' journals, trying to find someone who might have known my father, even a little. After a couple of weeks a pile of papers arrives from the National Archives: Attestation Form, Service and Casualty Form, Proceedings for Discharge, Determination of Demobilization Priority, Medal Awards Listing. This is what is left of four years of war, from the moment on 11 February 1942 when my father walked between the sombre grey columns of the Melbourne Town Hall into the cavernous tiled room filled with desks and tables, until the day in April 1946 when he folded up his small pile of khaki clothing, belt, and boots, and handed them in at the quartermaster's window. The forms do not tell stories—they only ask questions.

Somewhere between a cold port on the Baltic and the booth where he filled in his form, Stanislaw was transformed into Stanley. Was this the decision he came to while sitting on the steps of the Town Hall in 1939, going back day after day in his desperation to enlist—to be told that as an alien without Australian citizenship he would have to wait until he turned twenty-one—or twenty-one and five-twelfths, as he has entered on the form. And there is this extra five-twelfths to explain, also—why, given his impatience, he waited five months after his birthday before going to enlist. His occupation is entered as 'Cutter'. Was this perhaps a simplification of the series of odd jobs he had taken since arriving in 1937, among the close-knit Jewish community in Carlton and St Kilda—making handbags with his uncle Leon, beginning a lampshade-making business with some young friends?

Such uncertainty may have provided another good reason for joining up. With unemployment running at ten per cent, the 'five-bob-a-day' offered by the Australian Imperial Forces represented a low but steady income, with no extra expenses for food and shelter. And—perhaps a sign of his feeling of safety in his new country, perhaps even a clue to his determination to enlist in the army of a country of which he was not yet a citizen—he chose to write 'Jewish' in confident, flowing letters, despite the 'Answer optional' appended tactfully after the question. Under 'Technical qualifications' he listed only '4 languages': French, which he had learned as a child with Mademoiselle Felicia; Polish and Yiddish, which he had spoken at home in Warsaw; and English.

The forms provide a skeletal outline of where he went after filling out the form—off to a cold room for the army medical examination, which certified him as fit, but only for Class IIA service because of his short-sightedness. Class IIA duties—that is, 'specified duties in any unit in which the disability is no bar'—

might mean driving a field ambulance, carrying stretchers, or working at headquarters. Did he rejoice or lament at being spared from the killing itself? At the AIF Details Depot in Caulfield he took the Oath of Enlistment, but a line through the blank space after 'I ...' suggests he was allowed to make a simple affirmation of allegiance in place of the oath, which ends with the words, 'So Help Me God'. There is only one unassailable fact: he was assigned the rank of private in the army, number vx75111.

Leafing further through the pile, I come to the Service and Casualty forms, the comprehensive record of his four years of army service. They are covered with information that is typewritten, stamped, or scrawled in a variety of hands. They are like a mirror of the cramped, disciplinary life of the army, a strange—and perhaps even comforting—contrast to the chaotic, terrifying experiences that lay ahead. From the Details Depot, Private vx75111 was transferred to the AAMC Depot in Wangaratta, after four days' leave without pay. He had only four days to say goodbye once again to the life he had been living— to his uncle Nathan's watchmaking shop in Collins Street, to the handbag factory, to extravagant theatrics at the Yiddish Kadimah, and to painting lampshades in a bungalow with the brilliant young artist Yosl Bergner.

After three months in Wangaratta come a series of entries.

Offence: AWL 2200 hrs 9/5/42 to 2200 hrs 10/5/42. *Award:* 4 Days CB & Forfeit 1 Days pay.

Offence: Failed to appear at place of Parade Appointed by his C/O 26/5/42. *Award:* 3 Days CB.

I think of my father in the training camp at Wangaratta— surrounded for the first time entirely by strangers, for month after month. Letters from his family in Warsaw had stopped coming. Although Anne and Mary, his cousins, wrote to him regularly from Melbourne, they could not tell him anything about the fate of his family. Ahead of him lay new countries and new conflicts, fighting amongst men who had lived a very different life. I wonder if these were the reasons for his inexplicable absences without leave, his failure to show up for parade. Or perhaps it was something more mundane—a late return from leave after too much carousing, a date with a local girl, a quarrel with another soldier, or simply a laxity of discipline.

In any case, the nature of the problems seems to have changed. The next entry, only two months later, transfers him with a stroke of the pen to the Sergeants' Camp in Watsonia. But there is no mention afterwards of a promotion—either the training was of some other kind, or it was unsuccessful. Poring over these entries written in crabbed handwriting, I wonder if someone chose my father on the basis of his qualities—his good humour and popularity, his conscientious style, his calm thoughtfulness—before some strange current emerged which told against him as a leader, as one who would stand out in the group. There is nothing here of a serious nature to indicate a rebel, a troublemaker, or a poor soldier. But he seems repeatedly to be chosen out, only to be passed over for some invisible reason. And most of all, periodically he simply seems to vanish. He is 'Absent Without Leave', or guilty of 'Failing to Appear', either for a few hours at a time or a full day at most. He is declared AWL 0630 hrs 4.4.43 to 2200 hrs 4.4.43, and fined one pound by C/O 2/3 Field Ambulance. On 11 May 1944 a charge of AWL is dismissed. On 20 December 1944 he is fined ten shillings for failing to appear at a place of parade. On 1 October 1945 he is fined three pounds for 'Conduct to prejudice of Good Order and Military Discipline'. In the next entry he is recorded as forfeiting his proficiency pay.

I try to read between these strange, alien entries, full of acronyms and abbreviations, authorities, documents, and dates, out into my father's life, but I am unable to see beyond these few tiny hills. On the other side, the terrain of the war—the Middle East, New Guinea, Borneo—spreads flat and uncharted, invisible to my eyes. Another form—his Proceedings for Discharge—gives me the raw facts of this time: 1511 days of war, 761 days in Australia, 688 days overseas. But when this document discharged Private Stanley Marin—Single, Age twenty-five years, Height 5 ft 5½ in.

Eyes Brown, Complexion Dark, Hair Black, Marks/Scars S.Back RHip—back onto the shores of his new country, had he changed? Or was he the same Stasiek who had leaned dreamily against the post on the Port Melbourne wharf, in his dark corduroy jacket and open-collared shirt, waiting, as so many of his people had waited before him, for a new life in a new country? Or was it a very different Stan Marin who stepped back onto the Melbourne pier in khaki drill that carried the dust of Cairo and the mud of Borneo in its fibres?

Rudi

After a few months, I begin to despair of ever tracking my father through those distant jungles, through the dunes of Egypt and the open-air markets of Cairo. It seems that the story of his war experiences will remain blank to me, the pages unfilled like so many chapters of my father's life. But one day I receive a letter in the mail, written in a looping, almost child-like hand.

> In reply to your letter in the Vet Affairs Journal, Vol 15 No 3 September 1999.
>
> I served with the 2/3 Field Ambulance 9th Div AIF as a Medic and a stretcher-bearer. And I knew Stan Marin, and all the rest in Head Qua. Company. I can remember him most clearly while on guard with him and my mate Blair Cunningham and my brother Stan Jaeger. I am Rudy Jaeger still going 81 years young and brother Stan is living in Busselton W.A. still young at 77. I do not know where or what happened to any of the names mentioned. Sorry I cannot be of any help, as we all went our different ways and different States.
>
> Yours faithfully
> (Rudi) Rudolph James Jaeger
>
> P.S. Perhaps some other mates can get in touch with you and let you know something (Are you a relation of Stan's?)

Joyfully, I write back to Rudi and, after a week or so, receive the first of a series of letters from which my father's life during the war begins to emerge like a photograph slowly developing in solution. In his letters Rudi seems almost grateful for the opportunity to recount this experience which so transformed his life and the lives of those around him. He conscientiously paints for me the colours of the war, the banality, the fear, the comedy and, from time to time, the strange wonder of night and silence or early mornings in a land so far from anything they had ever known. His letters are rambling, wonderful compositions, full of happy exaggerations and the most meticulous listings of incident and circumstance. He scatters humorous remarks in parentheses and pieces of extraneous wisdom in the margins and at the top of each page: next to a list of the men of his platoon he squeezes in the observation *By failing to prepare, you prepare to fail*; at the top of page 3, *Only the foolish and the dead never change their opinions*; and as a P.S. *We believed you cannot plough a field by turning it over in your mind*. This expansiveness, this humour and innocence, seems so distant from my father's grim and determined silence about the war that I wonder how the same experiences could have touched them so differently. But perhaps it is easier to unburden oneself to a stranger, across distance and in writing, than to face the enquiring looks in the faces of one's family.

Dear Bernard Marin

I am very glad to tell you what stories I know from your father, he was a quiet bloke, and kept to himself. He hated rifles or anything that took life. We had a few bludgers and losers on our unit, but I never heard one bad thing about Stan Marin—<u>he did all things well</u>. I can tell you that in New Guinea we would sometimes have to carry a jeep out of the mud, five of us on each side, and Stan Marin would be in there doing his best. 'A brave man is one who sees the danger, fears it, and yet meets it,' I always say, like Stan Marin. But that is something I can talk about later on, and now I will try to tell you the story as I saw it, though it is many years ago now (sometimes it doesn't seem hardly more than a day).

We (that is, the 2/3rd Field Ambulance AIF) were camped up at a station called Kildonan, near Goondiwindi doing exercises (with the sheep instead of the enemy, some jokers had it) when they sent us up the orders to ship to the Middle East. A bunch of us had got to be mates by that time—I will give you a list later, but there was my brother, Stan Jaeger, Blair Cunningham who enlisted together with me, and Stan Marin, your dad, and Norm Taylor. (I remember how my brother used to laugh at Stan Marin, because of the way he would ask for A Cup of Tea. My brother would say, No Stan, Cuppa tea, Stan, Cuppa tea. He would say it every time, and in the end he did learn to say it right) We marched a full day down to Bogabilla, but when we got there we couldn't see a whisker of the train, and the sky was turning purple over the flats. After a couple of hours, I said, Well, gents looks like we'll be sleeping here tonight. And one of the men said, What, here on the bloody ground? There was a lot of grumbling amongst the men, because we had to drink the bore water which was warm and a bit murky. (Time was to come when that night would be a very pleasant one to look back on.)

About five in the morning, we heard the hooting of the train and we scrambled for our packs, men bumping into each other in their hurry. (A lot of men wore glasses, that was why they were in the medics.) So we were a pretty ragged-looking bunch that climbed down off the train at Sydney. You know, some chaps had never seen the city before. We were feeling sort of pleased with ourselves, on a sunny morning, chests puffed out, marching through the Sydney streets to Woollomoloo. And then we got our first glimpse of the boat and our spirits sank to billy-o. She was rising up in front of us, the Aronda. Size 9,000 tons. Property of the British Indian Steamship Company, in big white letters on the side.

What a godforsaken 9,000 ton sardine can she was! and didn't smell much better, either.

As the last stragglers on board, we were left to string hammocks or bed down on pallets in the storage hold—it was like the Black Hole of Calcutta down there, damp and no air. One fellow said, 'Well, chaps, I'm off home,' and the lot of us laughed, but to tell you the truth, our hearts were in our boots.

What it was like in that ship, packed to the gills with men, as we turned down into the Southern Ocean around Tasmania (we couldn't go through the Strait as it was mined) I can't tell you. The waves would reach 25 feet high, and the ship would go right under them. Blair Cunningham came down from the deck, all white in the face, and he said, 'We were looking straight up into the waves, and I could see the bloody sharks.'

Going across the Bight, we were all pretty nervous—I thought to myself, there must be thousands of false teeth scattered all the way to Fremantle. Half the men couldn't stand up for seasickness, and the rest were on edge the whole time, and scraps broke out at the least provocation. So after a while they started locking us below most of the time. Down in our hold, with not even a porthole for a breath of fresh air, we played cards on the bunk for day after day, waiting to get to Fremantle. I asked Stan Marin how he got to be so good at cards. He said to me, Well, I did this journey once before, only coming the other way.

The sardine-tin was so battered by the time we reached port, that they had a full week's work to get her ship-shape again. For us, that week was like an hour to a hanged man—the breeze curling in from the bay, and the sea lapping gentle like a little puppy. Then, a day early, they packed us back on board, and the men's faces started to get that hunted look they had back in the Bight. And it was fair on for worse than before, because this time we knew too well what we were in for. As we pulled out of Fremantle, one fellow, not a young bloke, maybe in his thirties, climbed up on the rail with his yellow lifejacket on. He sat there for a minute and looked over his shoulder at the sea. You could see black fins in the distance, circling. He just turned and looked back at us and at the ship, then he fell backwards into the white wake of the ship. It was pretty quiet on the deck, nobody moved. Then someone called out, 'Bit cold for a swim, mate!' and everyone perked up a bit. A boat picked the fellow up out of the water after a bit, and took him back to Perth for a deal of trouble. But I'll tell you, a lot of men on that deck would gladly've followed him.

I must end here for the moment, as it is getting dark, and my eyes are not so good. I will try to write some more soon. I hope it is some use to you.

All the Best,
Rudi Jaeger

P.S. As you can see by my name, that it is German—my grandfather came out to Australia, 25 years before the first world war, long before Hitler and his followers. He was a good, hard working farmer, they reared 8 sons and 3 daughters.

It's not long, less than a couple of days, before I receive Rudi's next letter, with its painstaking, looping letters forming my address. It strikes me how extraordinary it is that this old man sits in Queensland writing down all of the things that he has carried with him for nearly sixty years, things that happened to him when he was just a young man, in a slouch hat, facing things I could barely imagine.

Dear Bernard

It's a pity you're not here for me to tell you the story in person. I keep worrying that I've left things out. If you don't mind, I will start again after that awful queasy voyage to Perth.

It was better when we got out in the open sea, pretty calm for a couple of weeks, steaming dead straight across the Indian Ocean. To the east, the whole Pacific was under the Japanese, since Singapore fell in February. That was when most of us had joined up—me and my brother—and your dad too, I think. We all knew Australia was next, likely as not. We looked east as we travelled, and spared a thought for the poor blokes on New Guinea, trying to keep the enemy out of Moresby. We didn't know then that it wouldn't be too long before we were there too.

Around us, the ocean looked calm, but there was danger below. One morning, we were woken up by the sound of the ship's horns blowing, and a change in our steady north-easterly route. One of our cruisers and a corvette were circling the ship, searching for the enemy below. We all stood watching from the ship's deck. Something flashed past to the stern , and a fellow called out, Torpedo! No-body could breathe while we waited to feel the dull thud, and the aftershock, and then the groan as the ship would start going down into the water. But the crunch didn't come, we could only hear the far away boom of depth charges searching out the submarine. Must've been a jet-propelled sea snail, Norm said.

By the time we stepped off onto the pier at Colombo (on Ceylon) Stan Marin, Jim Cunningham and I (we all had leave for a couple of days) our knees felt wobbly to have the solid ground under our feet. Jim said, Oh, I miss the rocking already, let's get back on the ship, and we all laughed. We walked about three paces before we were surrounded on all sides by rickshaw drivers, and every time we turned around there was another face saying, Rickshaw, Sahib? Rickshaw? Finally, we gave in, and got in a rickshaw each, but the drivers got into a fistfight, and suddenly took off in different directions. And I tell you, I had a few anxious moments all on my own in a strange city. I thought to myself, Well, I didn't last the whole journey across the bloody ocean to be dispatched by a bloody rickshaw wallah. Then all of a sudden we met up at the corner, and we all had the same look on our faces. I looked at them, and they looked at me, and the three of us just burst out laughing, and couldn't stop for about ten minutes, and the rickshaw fellows just stood there staring at us in consternation.

Well that's all for now. I will continue the story in the next letter.

Rudi Jaeger

I wait anxiously for the next letter, feeling as though I have left my father in the middle of his journey. In the intervening time I see Mum, and I ask her about Dad's letters, and whether he talked about his feelings and impressions. She sighs and says, 'No, only dates, places, things like that. It was hard during the war.'

A few days later, another letter arrives from Rudi.

Dear Bernard

It was with a glad heart that I got your letter of 20th November. I sent your letter to brother Stan in W.A. and he also remembers your father very fondly, especially the Cup of Tea. I'm sad to say that we lost my older brother, Mervyn, the other day. He was 86. He did not go to the war.

If I have told you this part already, sorry, as I did not keep a copy of what I have already sent you. We stopped overnight to coal up at Aden, at the neck of the Red Sea. We woke up the next day, and we were all covered in coal dust. Black all over. One fellow said, Good, now the enemy can't find us at night. But as it turned out it was more that we couldn't find our own, as we lost a man overboard that night on the way through the Red Sea. We steamed on up through the Canal to Port Said, where we were put on trucks to Gaza. We expected to be sent up to El Alamein, where Montgomery dealt the enemy such a stunning blow, but we weren't well-enough accustomed to the desert, so they sent us on to Tel Aviv, and Jaffa instead. We trained as stretcher-bearers in the hospitals around Palestine. Christmas of '42 we spent in Jerusalem, and then went on to Alexandria. On the way through the desert, we woke up one morning to find the whole valley covered with lilies which had flowered overnight. Norm said, 'It's a bleeding miracle.'

We didn't dare to go about at night in Alexandria—it was a very dirty and wicked city, and you would be robbed for sure. Some other blokes who had been there for some time told us that the local pickpockets would take not just your wallet, but your whole pocket, too. So we went around always in twos, carrying knives.

Soon we were travelling in a bug-infested train across the desert. The heat rose up off the desert like a wall, and shimmered with mirages that looked just like a lake in the distance. We stopped over and over, because the oil from the engines kept leaking onto the rails, so that the train couldn't move. We would have to hop off and shovel sand onto the rails to get the train going again. There were a lot of Arabs working next to the tracks to keep the road fair for the army, and some of the Aussies on the train would crush up a dog biscuit, very fine, and throw them out onto the sand, and the Arab boys would grab a handful of sand and pick out the small bits of biscuit—they were half-starved. Some other men would jump off and take melons from the Arabs who were trying to sell them, and then jump back on the train just as it was taking off. But one time, a chap who'd pinched two melons slipped on the sand getting into the train, and was left behind. So I guess that served him right.

After a while, it almost got to be like a game. The Arabs would steal whatever they could—even take our kitbags from under our heads while we were asleep. One chap woke up in the morning to find that his whole tent was gone from around him. They were a funny lot. One day we came to a road, and along came an Arab riding on a donkey, and his wife following on foot. We stopped him and asked why his wife was walking while he rode. He said, 'Oh, she has no donkey'.

It was pretty soon after this that the big push started, it was a massive effort, 400 guns firing at once, and replaced with another 400 when they got too hot. But we were part of the 9th Div. by then, and got posted back to New Guinea, travelling in convoy on a 45,000 tonner called the Acurtanier (not spelt right). I will tell you about this next time.

Well, I may not be able to write for a while, as I must go to W.A. for the funeral. Merry Xmas to all.

Rudi

During the long wait for another letter, I return again over the document of my father's war service. After the boisterous life of Rudi's letters, the beetle-tracks of numbers and abbreviations across the page seem frustrating, barren. But I can't help but try to fill in the grey areas that are left. I go back to the Service and Casualty list. 'Embarked Mid. East 24.1.43; disembarked Sydney 27.2.43.' Yet another journey across the world—a strange time for a young man in his twenties caught up in the inexorable tide of history. I wonder what he was thinking about on that journey home—to a home which only a few years before was a foreign, exotic destination. He had spent his Christmas in Jerusalem—but was it as a Jew, a Pole, an Australian, or simply as himself? Did he visit the Wailing Wall, where the Hasidim prayed with shaking fervour, did he speak to the hale young secular Zionists who were already planning a new state? What did it mean to be at the heart of his ancient identity, but in a borrowed guise, the uniform of another country, another continent? From Rudi's letters it seemed that the other men had little idea of his Jewishness, of any kind of difference except his quiet solitude and the absence of an Australian drawl, the too-perfect English he had learned in Warsaw.

The only answer to this question arrives in another package of documents from the National Archives—my father's naturalisation papers. It was just after he returned from Palestine that my father made his application for naturalisation as an Australian citizen. This meant renouncing his allegiance to Poland, swearing an oath of loyalty to the British Crown, and placing advertisements in the daily papers signalling his intention to become an Australian. In the file, there is a letter which attests to his determination.

> The Undersecretary
> Department of the Interior,
> Canberra
>
> Dear Sir,
>
> In July of this year I made application through the C.O. of my unit for naturalization. Since then I have heard no more of this matter. As I am desirous of having this finalized I would be glad if you would make enquiries and notify me how things are progressing,
>
> If you have not received my application, please forward another form.
>
> Yours faithfully
> S. Marin.

In his application, my father wrote his name as Stanley, not Stanislaw, which had to be added by the clerk. With the legendary efficiency of wartime bureaucracy, his certificate of naturalisation was issued in March 1944, a full year after the application was lodged.

Looking again at the documents, I remember the entry on his demobilisation form—Scars—S.Back R.Hip. Small of the back, Right Hip. A gash from playing soccer as a child, Mum told me. But there was another scar, on his forearm, from a tattoo that was removed after he married Mum. It was during the war that he had it done, one night, when he and a couple of his mates were very drunk—perhaps among the fleshpots of Alexandria. The white scar-tissue the tattoo left behind remained clearly visible on his arm until he died. As a child, I remember looking at the scar and wondering, but I knew never to ask my father about it.

At dinner one night, when she is visiting, I ask Mum about the tattoo. What was it—hearts and daggers, or a girl's name, or the platoon emblem?

'No,' Mum says. 'Of course not, don't be silly. Bernard, why do you want to know these things?'

'So what was it then?' I ask.

'If you must know,' she says, 'it was a map of Australia.'

Dad had requested an outline of the continent of Australia tattooed on his right forearm. As with so many other things in his life, what remained of this brave or foolhardy act of belonging was a pale, silent scar that never quite healed.

Late January brings a series of blazingly hot days on which the great open blue sky hangs overhead like the roof of a tent. It is too hot to work, too hot to think. But the heat that hangs before my eyes does not come off the thick asphalt and concrete of the Melbourne streets; it accompanies the shimmering haze of the desert sands, under the distant boom of the guns or the strange, abandoned silence. I wonder what changes the blazing heat forged in the Polish boy. I can almost feel my father changing, like tempered steel, in the crucible of the heat and the dust, the relentless blast of the desert wind searching out the last traces of water and softness. I know already that by this time he had ceased to receive any news from his family in Warsaw.

At last, another letter comes from Rudi. I tear the envelope open in my haste and excitement, and devour the pages quickly like a glutton before reading them over again more carefully.

Dear Bernard;

I am back home on the range after too long an absence, and enjoying the chance to sit down and write you some more of my story. I hope you are not getting bored by an old man's reminiscences. The funeral, and seeing my brother Stan again after some time brought much back to me. I want to write it all down as time is <u>getting short</u>.

I wrote to you last about the Middle East and our training there—by the time we left, we were not raw recruits any more, but getting used to the ways of war. But nothing could have prepared us for New Guinea. They gave us some jungle training, on the Atherton Tableland, but it was like taking swimming lessons in a sandpit. The worst danger in Queensland was running into a mad cassowary, but in New Guinea it was constant fear, day and night. Fighting in the desert was all open terrain—you could see the enemy a mile away, or the planes coming over. It was hairy, but you knew where the danger was, and what your chances were. In the jungle, you couldn't see the enemy if he was standing a few feet away: and oftentimes they were dug in underfoot, or hiding in the canopy overhead.

We landed at Milne Bay in early August of '43. The Aussies had pushed their way back up the track to Kokoda, taking a whack of casualties. When we walked into the clearing station there were wounded and dying everywhere. Blair Cunningham said to me, 'Bloody hell, it's like rush hour in Elizabeth Street ...' There was mud everywhere, up to your ankles—the tents were sinking down into it, even on the corduroy bases. The track to Lae was worse—the mud was up to our knees sometimes, it was raining heavily and crossing the rivers was getting more and more difficult.

On the way to Lae, we took a lot of casualties—the hospitals were crammed to breaking point. When we got to a new site to camp, we would spray the spot with petrol, and light it, to help kill the vermin, rats and such, and set up the tents for the hospital. We had to bring the wounded men back on stretchers—it was hard work, four men had to carry a stretcher for a long haul, and when night came the jungle became as black as the ace of spades, with rain and mud up to our knees. We couldn't see past our noses. The natives could see a bit better, and without them, we couldn't have made it—the fuzzy-wuzzy angels they used to be called. Some nights we had to sleep in the rain, sitting against a tree or laying on a log on the ground.

After a while, the Japs broke through again, and we demanded to have rifles to defend ourselves. At night we would try to sleep, but we were always afraid that someone was moving in the undergrowth, in the pitch darkness. One night, I was on guard along with the two Stans, your dad and my brother, and Blair Cunningham, and we heard a noise coming through the jungle. It started as a rattling and then got louder and louder, until something was crashing through the trees towards us. In a panic, we started firing, and suddenly a mob of wild pigs broke through into the clearing, and ran all over the camp—pigs were running in all directions, squealing and tripping and getting caught in the tents. We started to laugh so much that a couple of us was nearly sick—my brother Stan could hardly speak for nearly an hour, he was just shaking his head, and breaking out all over again.

Another quiet day in the jungle, all the blokes were having a well-earned rest. Of course, I was always playing jokes on them, and this particular day, Stan Marin and my brother Stan Jaeger broke open a couple of bullets and got out the cordite—if you burnt this it would go off like rifle shots. I took a handful of cordite and threw it into the fire, it jumps about as it goes off; and the men were out and had their helmets on in a flash. In those days I was a boxer and a wrestler, 6 foot, and weight 14 stone. They did not say much. I wonder why. Stan Marin really had a good laugh over this little joke.

No-one can really understand what it was like—at least not the same as one of those who were there. You never forget the cobbers who served with you—you couldn't have made it without your mates. Some days we would be walking single file up a river bed, about 20 feet apart, with enemy in the jungle on both sides. We would feel our hair standing up, we never knew when we would be next to cop a bullet. There was only your mates, and nothing else. You would hang onto them like grim death, and it was worst of all when one of them got it hard.

And pretty soon we did lose some blokes. One night we heard enemy planes coming over the mountain. We dived into a foxhole that the Japs had dug—it was a hole about six feet deep. I dived in first, and the two Stans dived in after me. Watch out, I told them, only one man to a grave. Then about four others dived in too, and I ended up like a sardine squashed under six other men all night, while the Jap pilot made passes over again and again, guns blazing. We lost three men and two wounded. So they put some new recruits into our unit—they had no experience in the jungle. And that's how it happened. One young fellow was on guard, it was about 100 degrees at night, and there was a pale moon shining down through the trees. James Cunningham and Norm Taylor, were sleeping on a makeshift bed of sticks and leaves. Norm Taylor turned over in his sleep and this young chap on guard thought it was a Jap helmet, and fired, and hit Norm – can you imagine waking up to this terrible thing. I was with the doctor in the operating tent at this time, when I heard a shot and a scream. Then I heard Jim Cunningham cry out, 'Don't shoot again, it's Norm, he's been shot!' I helped carry Norm into the doctor's tent.

He was losing a lot of blood. They were asking for someone with the right blood group, I said mine is O+, I want to give my blood. But next morning, Norm was sent away to hospital, and he died of the shock. For a long time, we were all very quiet, we didn't know what to say. I thought about it a lot—if I had been asleep instead of in the operating tent, it could have been me who was shot instead of Norm. I wondered why it was me who made it, and not him. He was only 27 years old. The young guy who fired his rifle never got over it, and they had to send him home.

After that, I can remember trying to sleep, and hearing noises in the jungle, and you would jump up with your rifle in your hand, still half asleep. Wild bananas grew in the jungle, and when the wind blew, the flapping of the banana leaves would wake us up, never got much sleep. The jungle is a very spooky place in wartime. No wonder a lot of men came out with bad nerves. Probably your dad did also. I know I did—took me 2 or 3 years to come good. And some never recover.

Once Lae was taken, the 9th Division was sent to capture Finschhaffen and Langemark Bay on the Huon Peninsula, fifty miles or so east of Lae. We landed north of the town at a place called Scarlet Beach. Before the landing, a Jap soldier was captured and they got him to talk. He told that the order was to annihilate every Australian and American at Scarlet Beach. So we got ready for them. When the Japanese attacked that night—there was a shipload out at sea coming in on barges, others came down on foot from Sattelberg.—our motor torpedo boats met them with blazing searchlights and machine guns and the 24th waited for them in the jungle if they made it to the beach.

If that Jap soldier had not told us the truth, we would have been wiped out. In the dead of night, torpedo boats were approaching the beach in a blaze of bullets; planes were flying over and dropping daisy-cutters (100-pound bombs that could slice clean through a coconut tree.) The black sky was lit up with flares and explosions, and men were diving off the boats into the water, trying to get away from the strafing fire from above. Hundreds were slaughtered in the bay and on the beach, it was red with blood. It was a miracle that any of us survived.

We were on the beach unloading equipment, when the Japs came over and fired on us, killing some American chaps. They came so low that I could see the eyes of the pilots. There was a hole dug in the bank, and hundreds of men were running to get in this hole, when a big, black American soldier yelled 'Move over snake and make room for one of your own kind!' For some reason, Stan (your dad) found that the funniest thing of all, and he liked the Yank for it, and they got to be mates. That's about the last thing I remember before we were pulled out of New Guinea.

Not long after Scarlet Beach, we were sent back home. We went on to Borneo, but I developed a bad foot and could not march, so I was left behind. At this time, brother Stan was boarded out with malaria, and so we went back to help on the farm when the war ended. I wonder what happened to all those men, we all went our different ways. Could you let me know when Stan Marin died and how old he was. I remember him as he was in New Guinea. He looked about 22 years of age then. He was a quiet bloke, but laughed a good deal, and he was good mates with all in the unit. It was a strange time, a long time ago, but I think of it often, and sometimes even now I wake up in the darkness of a morning, and I think I can hear the flapping of the leaves, and the far away booming of the artillery.

I wish—all the best.

Rudi Jaeger
(Remember friends, we are shaped and fashioned by what we love)

That is the last letter I receive from Rudi, though we speak on the phone several times later. But now that the story is told, there seems not much more to say—and I feel I should leave him to rest for a while. The sun through the tall palms ragged from gunfire, and the sloping shadows of the jungle rising at the edge of the white sand are what we share: it makes the petty details of ordinary life seem unreal, like a dream.

With Rudi's story at an end, I fear that the remainder of my father's war will disappear again into fragments scattered among the great blank landscapes of the archives. I can see that on March 1944 the 9th Division returned to Australia on a Dutch ship called the *Clip-Von-Tain* for twelve months' training on the Atherton Tableland in jungle fighting and amphibious landings. The record shows that Stan Marin took two weeks' leave through the Leave and Transfer Depot from 15 March 1944.

A few weeks later, my mother calls and asks me to take her to a funeral. We're sitting at the back of the church, listening to the eulogy.

'Les, my father, had a good and undistinguished war,' Robert begins. 'Because of the ruptured eardrum and hernia, he was classified as a non-combatant soldier. In '89 we went back to Sabah on Borneo together, and twice local blokes came up to me and asked if my father had fought the Japanese. I told them "Yes—he was on Labuan." On each occasion they said to Les, "Thank you for saving us from the Japanese." On these occasions, Les became very awkward and bewildered because he thought he really did nothing.'

I had known Les Anderson as my father's gambling partner. Only now did I begin to understand the crucible which had forged such a friendship, which seemed to hang on through decade after decade. At the wake, I begin chatting to another old soldier, a tall man with white hair and smart, dark-blue suit, who knew Les and my father on Borneo.

'You know, by that stage,' he says, 'our worst enemy was malaria—your dad had it pretty bad, and when he got out of hospital, he joined up with us at the 2/1st Clearing Station, on the way to Borneo. The war was over in Europe, but we were still slogging on in the islands. In May '45 we rehearsed the landings on Borneo in Morotai—but in the end the rehearsal was worse than the real thing. To be honest, we were just waiting for it all to be over. We were stuck on that bloody ship for two weeks doing nothing, trying to sleep in shifts, sandwiched between the landing gear and the tanks. There was a lot of waiting—sometimes it's worse than fighting. Les and your dad saved everyone from going bonkers in the heat and the boredom and the stale air with their gambling ventures. First they started a Two-Up school down in the hull. It was pretty small stuff, but a lot of fun. Then they started an S.P. bookmaking on Boat Races (using what beer we had) below deck. It kept us occupied—we didn't even mind losing all our army pay. He was quite a character, your dad—I don't think there's one man amongst the 2/1st who doesn't remember him.'

We are swept apart by the tide of people moving around in the room. I think about what he has said, and wonder what strange alchemy transformed my father from the quiet twenty-two-year-old immigrant who boarded the *Aronda* in Sydney into the brash, confident Australian soldier, with his tattoo and his gambling, who arrived in Brisbane on 16 February 1946.

On the way home, I tell Mum about Rudi's letters, and the things I have learned about the war.

'Did you ever ask him about that?' I ask.

'He didn't like to talk about it,' Mum says. 'He told me a couple of things, but that was all. I remember, on Borneo, he said that the surgeons would laugh and joke while they were sewing up the soldiers and amputating limbs. And once he told me that he saw a man go troppo, put a handkerchief on his head and run into the enemy fire.'

'But didn't you want to know more?' I insist.

'Bernard, you don't understand,' she says. 'We had other things to worry about then. Plenty of things.'

We drive in silence for a while. Then I ask, 'How's Nellie?'

'Oh, haven't you heard? She's back at Montefiore. She's much better.'

'I might go and see her then.'

'Yes, I'm sure she'd like that. But don't tire her out. You and your questions.'

Just as she's getting out of the car, she fumbles in her bag, and gives me a folded-up, yellowed piece of paper.

'Perhaps you'd better have this, then,' she says hurriedly.

'What is it?'

'Oh, nothing, just something I have had in my purse, for … oh for far too long. I don't need it.'

It is a small newspaper article, in tiny print.

Stretcher Bearers' Prodigious Feats

The Doctors speak in the highest terms of the work being done by stretcher bearers who carry wounded from the battle areas sometimes under mortar and shell file. Two of these heroic stretcher bearers have been killed and four wounded. The stretcher bearers follow on the heels of the medical staff and 'leap frog' from one forward position to another as our advance continues. The unit is so well organised that the medical station can be put in full working order in less than 24 hours. Stretcher bearers who have done a notable job since the landing are Pte. Stan Marin, South Caulfield, who was born in Warsaw, Poland. Since Warsaw was razed to the ground by Nazi bombers, Marin has not heard a word from his mother, brother and sister. Then there are Corporal Joe Norris, Cairns, Qld; Pte. Jack Tuttle, Preston, Vic; Ptes Stan and Ruddy Jaeger, brothers, Qld; Pte John Wall, Tasmania; Pte Jack Featherstone, Melbourne.

I stare at this tiny document. Has my mother really carried it in her purse for fifty-seven years? Perhaps this is how the past is smuggled around, in people's purses, and in their hearts, no matter how long ago and far away it may seem.

Mila 16

Nellie snorts at the flowers I've brought her.

'Hmph,' she says. 'So you've come for the rest of the story, I suppose.' She waves me away. 'Put them in the vase, over there. I'll cut them later.'

'If you're not up to it, Nellie …' I say.

'I may be dying,' she says flatly, 'but I'm not dead yet. Go on then, ask me before you burst. '

'I wanted to know what happened to Dad's family after he left.'

'It's not so easy, Bernard. I only know little bits and pieces. You don't understand. Most of the ones who stayed didn't come out alive. And the ones who did make it, they didn't always talk about the things they saw. So we had to make do with what we heard.'

'Anything,' I say. 'Anything you can tell me.'

She begins with my father's departure from Warsaw.

On an April night in 1937, a party gathered in a small apartment in the heart of Jewish Warsaw. It must have been a subdued occasion, the mood a little sombre. In physical terms, it was not far from the apartment on Ogradowa, where Pinkus and Sara Marin had lived less than four years earlier, but in social terms it was a long and terrible journey away. The apartment on Ogrodowa was gone, swallowed up by the crises that followed the crash of 1929.

Pinkus's luxurious, imported fabrics, the cambrics and faille and duchesse satins, were no longer in demand as money became scarcer and wallets tighter. On the streets the mood had changed. The elusive feeling of common nationality and prosperity had withered under the cold hand of want, and the fragile new nation's protector, the defender of the Jews, Josef Pilsudski, had been carried on his bier through the streets of Warsaw before crowds of thousands in hysterical silence. At the universities, Jews were set a quota and forced to sit on ghetto benches; government contracts were no longer awarded to Jews; and the anti-Semitic *Endecja* grew larger every day.

But the small apartment on Mila Street, in the tenement building once owned by my grandfather, was filled that night with the sound of people talking and telling stories and clinking glasses. Sara had kept some of her beloved crystal, despite Pinkus's frequent gambling losses which caused such raging arguments between the two. And Pinkus's brother Julian had returned with his wife Ruth from Paris, for fear of losing their Polish passports; they had come to the apartment for the special occasion. The mood of melancholy in the air did not arise from the problems of the present, but from those of the future. Stasiek, now a sixteen-year-old, was about to set off on the long, unimaginable sea journey to Australia. What were the thoughts of these people as they watched their youngest child sail away to a faraway continent? I think of my own children, and I cannot imagine.

Nellie finishes this story, and she asks me to get her a glass of water. I tell her to stop if she is tired, but her voice continues to tinkle and creak in the dusty air. She begins to tell what she has heard of the last days of Jewish Warsaw. As she speaks, a picture arises from the past—a picture drawn from my reading, from the faces of my father's family in the pictures I have seen, and from the few, sparse details that Nellie is able to give me. This is what I see.

16 May 1943. On Mila Street, in what was once the Warsaw ghetto, a huge, desolate pile of bricks lies broken and charred under the morning sun. Occasionally perhaps, a stretch of cratered pavement is recognisable, a door-frame, or there, in amongst the rubble of dirt and bricks, a chipped, bottomless black pot, half of a thin mattress, a fragment of cracked mirror reflecting the grey sky, some dirty shreds of paper, or a yellowed photograph amongst the rubbish in a broken gutter. A light powder of ash and dust still floats in the air, settling in a thin, undisturbed layer over everything like a shroud. The only sound is the flapping of a poster on a lone section of wall left standing at the edge of what was once a great row of apartment houses.

The acrid smell of burning comes from afar, as the last timbers of the great Tlomackie Synagogue crack and fall, bitten to the heart by the flames. A dead, hollow silence fills the air, floating down from the empty grey square of the Umschlagplatz, near where the train tracks run like branching veins into the big world, and the ghetto gate where half a million thin feet passed on their way to nowhere.

This was once Mila Street. A pile of blackened bricks is all that is left of the apartment where, only six years before—or it might be a thousand—a small party gathered to farewell their youngest son, at a time when leaving this place was still a sadness and not a deliverance. The clink of glasses ceased to be heard here long ago, along with so many other sounds: the laughter of children; the shy giggle of Gutka Marin having her photograph taken with an earnest-faced, mousy-haired young man; the scribbling of Beniek studying for his engineering exams; even the arguments of Pinkus and Sara over his gambling debts, her new purchases on credit.

These ordinary human joys and pains died long before the ghetto itself died. They were replaced by the endless, attentive silence of the fearful, a silence which rose even over the ugly din of streets choked with starving people.

Now it all seems over, obliterated forever under the artillery which finally battered Jewish Warsaw into the ground. The last few thousand of the half million Jews left in the ghetto at last refused to walk the few blocks to the Umschlagplatz at the railway station, refused to hide in the airless bunkers where so many had died slowly of asphyxiation, and chose instead to pit a handful of meagre revolvers against a fully equipped modern army. They held out for almost a month. Their headquarters was next door, at Mila 18, an address now carved into history. Near the door where Sara and Pinkus, and Ben and Gutka Marin, came in and went out, and through which my father, Stasiek, walked when he left Warsaw for the last time, the heroes of the resistance, Mordechai Anelewicz and Joseph Lewartowski, fought the last desperate battle of an unwinnable, unforgettable uprising. And so it was Mila Street which bore the brunt of the inexorable German vengeance. The last fragments of wall now grin from the ruins like blackened teeth closing over the story of my father's family, the disappeared.

The last date on which we know anything for certain about the lives of the Marin family of Warsaw is 6 September 1939. Everything afterwards is chaos, conjecture. Thousands of young men left the city on the night of 6 September, under the orders of General Umiatowski who, at 11pm, his voice cracking with strain, acknowledged the city's defeat over the radio. They fled east across the river Bug and into the Russian zone. Among them was Beniek Marin, and his sister Gutka and her future husband. Before leaving, Beniek phoned his uncle Julian and asked him to join their group. Julian could not abandon his wife, Ruth, and they stayed together until they were parted finally by death. Sara, too, stayed in Warsaw through the terrible years that followed, until her story ended somewhere in the streets of the ghetto. Beniek and Gutka and their friends left the burning city, through the whirr of the falling incendiary bombs, the groaning hum of the bombers overhead, and the smoke and chaos in the streets. They crossed over the Bug, and travelled on further, to Vilno in Lithuania, the second Jewish city of Europe after Warsaw, and now within the Soviet sphere of influence. After that, we lose their trace, although there is a photograph of Gutka with a young man, probably her husband, dated 1940. We do not know where it was taken.

In Warsaw, the bombing, and the fires which lit up the night sky, continued for many days. On the eve of Jewish New Year, 13 September, the bombing was directed at the heart of Jewish Warsaw—Wolynska, Franciskanska, Nalewki Street. The few gravediggers left at the Zydowski cemetery could not keep up with the dead. In those first days, a proper Jewish burial still seemed the sacred right of the dead. Then, one afternoon, a long black car drove up to the cemetery gates for the first time. A German officer spat orders from the half-open window. 'All these carcasses must be interred within twenty-four hours,' he barked contemptuously. 'If this order is not carried out, you can all look forward to the firing squad.' Terrified, the gravediggers were forced to throw the bodies into the trenches dug for the defence of the city.

In October, the Jews of Warsaw began to see the outlines of the fate that was in store for them at German hands. Trucks rolled through the streets, picking up men and women for slave labour. The damage to the city was to be repaired, and it was the Jews who were to do the punishing work, regardless of age or strength: young men and women, elderly rabbis, children hardly old enough to be out of school, women in fur coats, businessmen grabbed on their way to work, thousands of people every day, sweeping and scrubbing the streets, carrying bricks of shattered walls, building factories for the German businessmen rolling into the city every day, until the life of the quarter groaned and cracked under the intolerable pressure.

In November, the murders began. At Nalewki 9, after the shooting of a policeman, the police rounded up fifty-three men from the apartment building and ordered them to dig their own graves. Almost every day bloody patches appeared on the sidewalks from shootings during the night. News began to filter into the city about the murders and deportations occurring in the outlying villages and towns. Makeshift shelters, in synagogues and public buildings, were set up for the waves of refugees flowing into Warsaw. On 30 November, an edict was issued ordering every Jew over the age of twelve to wear a white armband with a blue star of David on the right sleeve. In January, two hundred and fifty intellectuals were rounded up and killed in retaliation for the escape of a Jewish youngster involved in the Polish underground movement. In June, Jews were forbidden from certain city streets—the great north-south thoroughfare of Ujazdowskie and Napoleon Square.

Then, on the day of Yom Kippur, 1940, at 2.00pm, the loudspeakers crackled into life throughout the city, announcing that the city would be permanently divided into Polish, German, and Jewish precincts. By 30 October, all Jews in Warsaw were ordered to move into the already crowded quarter north of Sienna Street and east of the cemetery. Thousands could be seen every day over the next weeks, carrying a few meagre suitcases across the bridge from Praga, walking north along Zelazna or east along Leszno Street. In the first weeks of November, the foot traffic flowed the opposite way, as all Christians were expelled from the quarter. On 15 November, German gendarmes took up their posts at the entry points. The rich, sprawling Jewish quarter was jammed between the high walls of a closed ghetto; Jews could come and go only through the ghetto gates. Food became scarcer and scarcer—it could come into the ghetto only through the holes in its walls, where policemen were paid to look the other way as children scrambled through, a few potatoes thrust under their small coats. No-one could tell when life would be forfeit to the accident of a substitute policeman, or a sudden crackdown on the life-giving traffic through the ghetto wall. The population of the ghetto, swollen by refugees, surged toward half a million, in an area of only 425 acres.

Sara Marin lived through all of this. When Beniek and Gutka left for Vilno, she had remained behind in Warsaw—under what conditions, it is impossible to know. We can be sure that the apartment itself was slowly emptied of its contents: the clothes and trinkets, the pots and pans and feather mattresses, the tobacco pouch and pipes, the crystal from the dresser, the books in Polish and French and Hebrew, the remaining jewellery in the small box on the dresser. All were exchanged for food, to wrest another day from the clutches of starvation.

On the streets, the same thing was happening. Every tree, every wooden post or fence, went for fuel in the terrible winters, and no birdsong could be heard any more. To live without work was impossible—one had to find some employment in a factory, perhaps in a German concern operating outside the ghetto. Hurrying through the streets before dawn with thousands of others, in a din of clogs and thin shoes against the cobbles, one would notice the windows onto the street sealed up on pain of execution, trapping those inside in airless, dim, cramped rooms. One would smell the stench of starving, despairing humanity that hung in the air. In winter, more bodies would be lying in the streets. The workers would hurry on, hardly noticing them any more. Children hid in doorways until dawn, returning from the cemetery where they had scaled the wall to the Aryan side to sell some article and buy some food for starving families.

On a summer evening, returning from work before the curfew, one would see the crush of all kinds of humanity that swelled the ghetto. Some people were still able to afford a meal at Szulc's restaurant on Leszno and Nowolipki, or a ballet performance at the Melody Palace. Others haunted the streets like ghosts, while children picked through rubbish or propped themselves against a wall with the impassive stare of the starving. Life and death were brought into the open: men and women argued in the street; prostitutes lurched past doctors who were hurrying to tend the sick; the tireless workers from the orphanage on Sliska Street passed women removing clothing from men who had just died.

One evening, sometime in 1940, it seems that Sara Marin, my grandmother, was on the street past the curfew hour. Perhaps she was late returning from work, or was engaged in some transaction for food, or was caught outside for a hundred other trivial reasons. Whatever it was that brought her outside after nine o'clock, it also brought her death—at the hands of a German gendarme who, seeing another Jew breaking the ghetto laws, simply raised the gun, took aim, and fired; or perhaps she was rounded up with other curfew-breakers and taken to the Pawiak prison. Her death, which at any other time might have brought grief and sadness for so many people, now is simply swallowed up in the great black tide sweeping through Warsaw, through Poland, through Europe from west to east, as though flooding up through that great river of light and life which had once flowed out of this city, breaking its banks, and erasing its course forever.

Elsewhere in the city there is silence. Not even a *dorozka* clatters mournfully through the streets that night. The trams that turned screeching along the crowded boulevards seem to have stopped. Warsaw is silent.

Far away, on the border of the Russian zone, the soldiers prepare for an assault of a brutality never seen in human history. Within a few weeks, the murders of Jews, —first men, and then women and children—will have reached tens of thousands every day, until it becomes clear that a death sentence has been passed over every Jew still living in Europe. Vilno, the beautiful city of the Jewish renaissance, with its synagogues and yeshivas, its Yiddish poets and musicians, and its Institute for Jewish Culture and Learning, is to be stained with Jewish blood. In the Ponary forest, five thousand Jewish men are killed by the Germans and their Lithuanian collaborators in scenes of inconceivable barbarity. In nearby Kovno, a Lithuanian nationalist stands atop a pile of bodies bludgeoned to death with crowbars, and plays the national anthem on his accordion. Even the Germans are shocked. To avoid such bloody incidents, they begin to build the factories of death whose smoke is to befoul the world forever: Chelmno, Belzec, Sobibor, Treblinka, Majdanek, Auschwitz-Birkenau.

Somewhere in the east, perhaps in the city of Vilno, or in the countryside near the river Bug, or in a camp—Treblinka, or Auschwitz—or in a city street back in Warsaw, my father's brother and sister disappear forever, without a trace. Perhaps someone sees them die, takes a final message. Perhaps somewhere there is a letter or a document which records their names: Beniek Marin, 30, Gutka Marin, 25. But these deaths do not go unrecorded, unremembered.

I wish to remember them.

Jewish Warsaw is gone, erased forever: Ogrodowa, Mila, the shops on Nalewki St and the cloth warehouses on Gesia, the murmuring *cheders*, the Yiddish theatre, and the orphanage. And on the day the uprising ends, as a final gesture, the Germans set fire to the great synagogue where Stasiek Marin, Sara's small son, once stood at the richly decorated bima to read the *parashah* for his *barmitzvah*, with his father standing beside him. 'He brought us to this place,' he would have read, from the chapter *Ki Tavo,* almost at the very end of the Torah, 'and gave us this land, a land flowing with milk and honey.' It is a vision rich with life and fulfilment, the journey's ending. But the chapter ends with a terrible warning: 'The life you face shall be precarious: you shall be in terror night and day with no assurance of survival. In the morning you shall say, "If only it were evening!" And in the evening you shall say, "If only it were morning!" because of what your heart shall dread and your eyes shall see.'

My father's eyes were spared all of this—the black cart that came to pick up bodies in the early hours of the morning, the hastily dug pit, the thin covering of earth, shivering, naked people, children crying. But his heart? Did his heart know that dread in the morning and the evening? Did his heart die, too, extinguished by these days and nights of terror, and the hard, cold silence that followed?

Stan Marin, front row, third from the right, at a convention for S.P. bookmakers in the early 1930s

Part Three

The Bridge

'Well, thank God it's all over at last,' Wendy says, when I show her everything that I've discovered in the past months—my interview with Nellie, the letters from Rudi, the photographs, the family tree.

'Over?' I say. She looks at me calmly.

'Now we can get back to normal again,' she says.

'I suppose so. There's one last thing I want to do, though.'

'Oh God, no …' she says. 'Please don't tell me you're going to Poland.'

'No,' I say. She looks pointedly relieved.

'I want to write a book,' I say.

'Why?' She arches an eyebrow. 'You don't know the first thing about writing a book.'

'Why not? I've written one book already.'

'The accounting book? I thought that was your final-year thesis.'

'Yes, but I rewrote it and had it published.'

'What is your obsession with this stuff? It's a bit morbid, don't you think?'

'I want to do it for the family. I want to write it down for the girls so they'll always have it. So they won't suffer from this same silence I had to struggle against.'

'Oh, I think you're exaggerating. They're living in a different time. It's a completely different culture.' She smiles at me with her Anglo-Saxon composure. 'The past doesn't bother them as much as it seems to bother you.'

'It doesn't bother me, I just need to find out. I'm learning to grieve for my father, like Goldman says.' She rolls her eyes.

'That takes more than writing a book,' she says.

'And I think it's just as important for the girls as it has been for me. They should know about ...'

'Okay then.' She cuts me off short. 'If you feel you need to write a book for yourself, go ahead. Get it out of your system. You don't have to do it for our sake, that's all ...' She shrugs and goes on with her reading.

My father was born in 1920, in Warsaw, Poland, I begin. His father was a merchant. His parents belonged to the rich Jewish culture of Warsaw before the war. He had an older brother and sister, Beniek and Gutka, and a French governess, Felicia. His cousin Nellie lived with the family for much of her childhood.

I keep writing, and after a few pages, I stop and read over what I've written several times. I'm proud that so much of this story, which I thought was lost forever, is locked in black ink on the white page. I will write a book, I think, and this story will be kept somewhere, on a shelf. Pinkus and Sara and Rudi and Stan will never be left behind in the dust of history.

My father left Warsaw in 1937 and came to Australia, I continue. After working in a variety of jobs, in the migrant Jewish communities of Carlton and St Kilda, he joined the Australian army in 1942. I continue writing, excited by the thought of the book one day sitting on the bookshelf, and of my daughter's children taking it down off the shelf, and opening this door onto the past. Perhaps even a student in a library somewhere will use this book for their research. When I've written for an hour or so, I stop and look at what I've done. My hand feels rather cramped. And I am faintly worried by something.

My father ... the book begins. *My father was born in 1920 ... My father left Warsaw ... My father joined the army ...*

I put these thoughts out of my mind. I collect my work into a folder, and put it on the shelf in readiness to continue.

The following evening, after Wendy and the kids have gone to bed, I keep writing. And the next evening, too. And slowly the pages begin to mount up inside the lever-arch binder. Soon I find myself swept into the writing. Many evenings I look up and find it's almost midnight, and I know I will be red-eyed for a 7.00am conference the next day.

I am still seeing Dr Goldman regularly every week. I talk excitedly about my research and the book, glad to be able to demonstrate some positive progress.

'It's about my father,' I say. Dr Goldman nods. 'Well, about the family history, actually. All the research I've done. I'm putting it all down for my kids. It will enrich their lives. What greater gift can I give them?' I am talking excitedly.

'It will give them an insight into me, as well. I never had an insight into my father, and now I do. So I want to make it easier for them.'

'So you've discovered a great deal about your father, then?' Dr Goldman asks.

'Yes. I've never really thought of him in terms of the Holocaust. But now that I know what his family must have gone through, it makes everything else seem insignificant.'

Dr Goldman listens calmly.

'And it explains things for me. I mean, not only did he lose his family, but he went through all sorts of terrible things fighting in the war. He never spoke about any of it. So it seems like he was hiding all this trauma.'

'And that helps you feel less angry?'

'Yes. The war, the Holocaust. It explains so many things about my family, and about me, too. I've learned so much. I feel like I've finally penetrated the silence. I feel like I've arrived at the end of the journey.'

I sit in silence for a while. Dr Goldman watches me, his head bent slightly to the side.

'Actually, I have this mantra for myself,' I say. 'An immigrant at sixteen, fatherless at seventeen, an orphan at twenty, a soldier at twenty-one. I'm reprogramming my thought processes.'

'How are the headaches?' Dr Goldman asks

'I haven't had one for months. I'm sure you were right—it was all to do with my father, with my not grieving for him. Now that I've found out about what happened to him, the headaches have gone away. It's miraculous. Now all that's left is to close this chapter of my life, so I can move on. That's another reason for writing the book. So I have to thank you.'

'Mmm-hmmm,' Goldman grunts. He nods in his usual non-committal fashion. He could show a bit more appreciation of this success, I think to myself, but I don't say anything. We sit in silence. Oh well, I think, I'm happy that things are finally pulling themselves back together. I'll get on with the book.

A week or so later, I'm at the house in North Road. I'm putting back Dad's jacket that Mum lent me. Inside the cupboard I notice a bare telephone extension sticking out of the wall. I look around the house, and find four more outlets in various closets and niches, with no phones attached.

'Mum,' I say, 'why are there so many phone extensions in the house?'

'Oh, you know,' she says, vaguely. 'I don't need to use them anymore. I've got the portable phone now.'

'It's got something to do with Dad's gambling, hasn't it?'

Mum looks very nervous.

'Bernard,' she says in exasperation. 'You don't give up, do you? Why do you always have to be finding things out? Aren't some things best left alone?'

'Why did he need so many phones?'

'Oh, for God's sake!' she says, loudly. I'm surprised. She is usually very softly spoken.

'Okay, I'm sorry I asked,' I say, rolling my eyes. She looks a little embarrassed. I sit there in silence.

She makes some tea, and while we're drinking it she says, 'There's no mystery, Bernard.' She shakes her head, with a long-suffering expression on her face. 'Your father ran the bookmaking business from here for a little while. Until your grandfather put a stop to it.'

'Why did he run it from here?'

'Well, the police raided the building in Chapel Street. It was in all the papers, names and everything. So your dad and Reuben decided to set up here. Then one day I came home, and they were in the front room with some plain-clothed policemen. The police were waiting for the phone to ring so that they could collect evidence against Dad and Reuben, and charge them. But when the fellows rang up, and didn't hear voices they recognised, they would pretend it was a wrong number. That night Grandpa came over. He spoke to your dad for a while, and that was it. Stan came out looking very shame-faced. Pale as a ghost. I felt really bad for him. I never complained about the gambling, as long as it made him happy. And he was always careful.'

'What did Grandpa say to him?'

'I don't know, Bernard, I wasn't there.' She looks uncomfortable.

'So that was it with the gambling, then?'

'He did invest in a couple of racehorses. They were syndicated with some other fellows. We used to go down to the races at Flemington to see them run, and that was good fun, though it was very loud. He and Reuben moved the business out of here, but they got rid of it quite soon after that and bought the nurseries. And you know how he always loved cards. It was in him, the gambling, but he never let it take control of him, like some people, if you know what I mean.'

'What do you mean by "in him"?'

'That's it, Bernard, that's the whole story.' She begins clearing up the tea things.

I can tell she is not to be budged on this issue any further.

'Oh yeah,' Paul says. 'Don't you remember Dad's poker nights? They used to play every Friday night, at different houses. Every few weeks they'd have it at our place. Maybe you were too young back then.'

'No, I remember,' I say. 'Lying in bed, hearing the shouts of excitement from the den, muffled by the glass doors. It must have gone all night. And then, the next day, the stale tobacco fumes hanging around the house.'

'I used to go and pinch cakes and things that Mum made out of the kitchen,' Paul says. 'You did it once, but of course you got caught. Sometimes I went and watched the men playing cards. Dad looked happy. I remember thinking he'd be happy to die playing cards. And hey, he did, in the end.'

'I don't really get it,' I say. 'I don't understand this passion for gambling. He had a wife and family who loved him. But the only thing that made him happy was gambling. It's like a sickness.'

'It made him happy,' Paul says. 'What's wrong with that?'

'Well,' I say, 'I suppose you understand it better than me. You're a risk-taker. You're more like him.'

'Maybe. But, man, you should have seen the books he kept for his gambling. Immaculate. You would have been proud of them yourself. I looked at them once, when I came back from overseas—I stayed with them for a few days before I realised I couldn't stand it. Anyway, he was absolutely anal about keeping records. He had every single amount written down, for years and years—what he had bet, what he had won, the odds, everything. Who knows why? Bizarre.'

'Oh,' I say. 'That's not how I imagined it.'

'No?' Paul says. 'Well, it's always different from how you think. So …' He sits still for a moment, then jumps up in his usual abrupt fashion. 'I've got to go. Bye.'

When Paul has vanished, I sit and think about Dad's gambling. I might as well include it in the book. I get my telephone directory. Someone must know someone who shared this strange world with my father. I will not stop until I find a trace. I start calling everyone I know.

The Betting Shop

'No place for a Jewish boy,' wheezes Henry Feldman, sitting in a deep and rather ancient armchair in the lounge room of his red-brick house. 'That was what my old dad always said. Mind you, he ran the business, and he got me in there himself because I was quick with the accounts—I was a qualified engineer, you know—but he would always throw up his hands and say, 'Henry, Henry, what are you doing here? This ain't the business for a Jewish boy.' He was a funny one, old Isa.'

While Henry chortles to himself at the comic misdeeds of his dear departed father, I sit rather stiffly in the Jason recliner opposite, and take notes on the strange little world of my father's great passion. At 18 Chapel Street, East St Kilda, around 1952, were an array of ordinary ground-floor apartments such as might be found on any Melbourne residential street. However, on any given day one might see a large number of men, young and old, coming and going, for whom the usual comforts of these residences could not reasonably account. And every Saturday afternoon, well after the street itself had lapsed into the sleepy quiet of the weekend, a constant and frantic ringing of phones could be heard from the small back entrance—although it was somewhat muffled by the thick iron door to the top floor, which was securely locked all day and all night. The door only opened for a small number of men: some were rather snappily dressed; others bore the marks of work requiring a great deal of concentration and calculation.

Every day, my father, in his grey hounds-tooth jacket and brown fedora, must have climbed the stairs to the top floor of 18 Chapel Street. The great iron door opened into a long, dim corridor divided into a number of cubicles, perhaps six or eight, each containing two or three men, and an equal number of telephones. Every time one of the phones rang it was answered brusquely, and then quickly replaced, whereupon it immediately rang again. On Saturday afternoons all of the telephones were in use at the same time, so that the whole floor was awash with noise—a deafening, heart-quickening rush of phones, a constant murmuring and shouting, and the bustle of men dashing between cubicles. In each cubicle stood a blackboard, covered with figures which were written and erased with considerable frequency—7 to 1, £7; 8 to 3, £2 4s; 10 to 7, £1 5s 2d. This process created a sheen of white dust, and added a chalky taint to air already thick with cigarette smoke and after-shave. Next to the figures were a string of peculiar and original names: Sans Rival, Land Storm, Within, Jan Ferie, Great Event. Excited shouts could be heard, along with the turning of manual calculating machines and a scratchy, rather crackly intercom: 'Gross's got ten thou at eight to three on Goondiwindi. We're laying off two. Any takers?'

'Yeah, mate, I'll take a G at eight to three.'

'You can put Norm down for five Cs.'

'Okeydoke, five-oh-oh left on the table, who's gonna take it? Isa?'

'Oy, why not, you might as well ruin me, too.'

The crackling, ringing, shouting, grinding, and puffing would rise to a crescendo, and then, as the second hand on the clock ticked over to the starting time, the whole place would fall dead silent. The only sound would be the hissing static of the radio piped through a public-address system. The horses were at the blocks. Then a pistol-crack would set the race in motion. The race-caller's voice would begin quietly, insistently, like the sound of a chanting monk. Gradually it would increase in volume and urgency until it reached a breathless, almost hysterical pitch as the horses rounded the last turn. The hushed, smoky air of the top floor of 18 Chapel Street would be thick with excitement and expectation. Then all at once, as the horses edged past the winning post, the cacophony of the cubicles would break out again, a maelstrom of jangling telephones and rough, barking voices.

As Henry Feldman remembers all of this, he rocks with laughter, his heavy frame working itself deeper and deeper into the folds of the copious armchair until it seems he will be quite swallowed up by it. His mood seems to vary considerably, with inexplicably cheerful spells followed by equally inexplicable and grim depressions.

'Who owned the building?' I ask.

'Ha!' Henry says. 'Only the mayor of St Kilda! That was the word about, at any rate. He put in the iron door between the first and second floors, so we could lock out any snoopers. It wasn't exactly *above board*, if y'know what I mean. Which is to say, it was likely to get you a couple of years at Her Majesty's pleasure. 'Coz to be a bookie you had to have a licence, and you could only get a licence if you worked at the racetrack. But the bookies on the course could change the odds depending on how much dough was bet. Y'get me?' I nod, after a little deliberation.

'So what was the point of putting a lot of dough on a horse? If you did, the odds would change, and there goes your winnings. So that's why you had to have the S.P. bookie—Starting Price bookie, that is. You'd call us up on the blower, and we would take bets at the odds at the start of the race and pay out on that, fair and square. So you'd do a whole lot better with us. And what's more, you'd get a 10-per-cent credit off a losing bet into the bargain, no questions asked.'

'So, how big were the stakes? A hundred pounds? Two hundred?'

'A hundred pounds? Ha!' he splutters. 'We had one fella, name of Morry Gross, once he put sixty thousand on the win. Nearly sent the lot of us down the gurgler.' Henry folds his arms and stares at me glumly.

'Sixty thousand pounds?' I am amazed. 'How could you cover a stake like that?'

'Well, some of us would never go that high; we put a ceiling on the bets we would take. But your dad and Reuben, boy, they were crazy. They'd really go to the limit. There was a word or two around that they had another backer. But, anyway, we had a system of layoffs, so if you couldn't cover the bet you'd lay off part of the stake with the other bookies. That meant you had to be bloody quick on your feet to do the sums before the race started. And that's where your dad came in—just about the quickest head for figures I ever saw.'

I think about my father, and the intoxication of winning or losing tens of thousands of pounds in a couple of minutes, at a time when the average wage was ten pounds a week.

'How could you rely on people to pay?' I ask. 'You didn't have the money on the table.'

'It was a different world, son. We never had to put nothing in writing. We all knew each other—your word was your bond, like—the punters, the bookies, the bank, everybody. We used to all meet up at the cafe on the corner of Russell and Bourke every Friday arvo, and then we'd settle up. On occasion a fella would be stuck for the money, but we knew him, so that was all right, and he'd give us a post-dated cheque so we could cash it later on. The manager of the Commercial Bank of Australia was one of our regulars, and the Rozen brothers from Normans across the road. We were like a club; everybody knew everybody. And what we all knew was racing. We loved the thrill of it—the quiet just before the horses thunder across the line, your heart in your fist, waiting to see if you're lifted up in the clouds or thrown to the bloody wolves. Tens of thousands of pounds. It's really something.' He looks at me with wild excitement, then his face sags. 'It's all different now, a'course. Don't bother much these days.'

'What about my dad?' I ask. 'How did he fit in?'

'Your dad? Oh, he was a character. That accent, and his stories.'

'Did he talk about us? His family?'

'No, not really. Talked about racing, mostly. You didn't get into that sort of thing. Different world.'

'I guess, with all the excitement, you don't think about anything else?'

'You can't. It's a bloody buzz. Partly the danger of it, too. The police, they were always snooping around, trying to catch us in the act. But, to tell you the truth, they weren't much of an operation, those blokes. And there were a few of the boys in blue who liked a bit of a flutter themselves, same as anyone else. All you had to do was slip them a quiet fifty every now and then, and she's apples. Without keeping the cops pretty there wasn't much hope for a business like ours. But it's always the way. Things change, and there's no respect for the way it's always been done.' Henry glares at me furiously. Then his mood changes again, and he chortles.

'But my dad, bless 'is soul, old Isa, had a sixth sense for trouble. "Henry," he said, "The writing's on the wall. Time to get ourselves a beach view." It wasn't much to shift—we never kept any files or anything what could get us in trouble. A morning's work, and we were down in Beaconsfield Parade. Sure enough, it can't have been more than two weeks later when Chapel Street got a little visit from the law. They couldn't get up the stairs 'coz of that nice big door, so they had to climb in the window. What a sight! Most of them had beer bellies on them like nobody's business, trying to squeeze themselves in off the ladder. Old Isa said, "What a bunch of *meshuggeners!*"'

Henry is wheezing with laughter again, working himself dangerously into the folds of the armchair.

'Your dad was there, a'course,' Henry continues. 'Told me he stuck his head out the window, an' what did he see but a policeman scaling the wall of the apartment block next door, trying to get a look at what was going on inside. Then he fell through the window, and someone screamed, "Throw the bastard out!" But it was too late. They were all taken down to the local constabulary and charged. Your dad and Reuben got in Ray Dunn, who was a mate of ours. But next morning they were splashed all over the front page of *The Herald*.'

'So was that the end of Dad's career as a bookie?' I ask. Henry wheezes again.

'Eh-heh, not then, no,' he says. 'They moved the business to your house. Did pretty well, too. Oh, he was a character, your father. He'd take risks more than any of the other fellas, Reuben included. Isa used to say, "Stan's a *mensch*—a prince among gamblers." And he was doing well, living pretty high with all of it. Bought himself a couple of horses, and did well with them, too. But then, I dunno, he just let it all go.'

'Why?'

'I dunno,' he says. 'Maybe your mum didn't like it.'

'I never understood it,' I say. 'Why he loved it so much. He seemed to love it more than his family.'

Henry looks uncomfortable, and shifts around in his armchair, pulling himself out of the enveloping folds.

'It's a hard one to explain. There are lots of reasons to love it—excitement, mates, money. It was quite a world. But he gave it up in the end, after all.'

'So why did he give it up?' I ask. 'Maybe he shouldn't have. It seems like the only thing he ever really loved.'

'I can't tell you nothing more than that,' Henry says. 'I wasn't there. Go see Reuben Solomon. Maybe he can tell you something.'

'I thought about doing that, but I'm not sure. My dad didn't speak to him for twenty years. I feel disloyal.'

'Awwww.' Henry waves his hand at me. 'Time to bury the hatchet, then, eh? If you want to know about Stan, that is.'

The Dead

The telephone rings very early in the morning, just as I'm about to leave the house. Wendy answers in the other room, and I hear the faint sounds of a quiet conversation on my way out. I'm getting into the car when Wendy calls me from the front step. She hands me the cordless, and I take the call, standing in the driveway next to the car. A voice says, 'Bernard? It's Sonia.'

It is John Weisman's daughter.

'How are you?' I ask. 'How's your dad?'

'Well, not so good, actually,' she says. 'I'm calling from the hospital. It looks pretty bad. The doctors don't expect him to survive more than a few hours. I just wanted to let you know.'

There is a silence on the phone. What is there to say?

'I had no idea,' I say. 'We went skiing a couple of months ago. And I spoke to him last week.'

'Yes, it has been a shock. He's been bad for a couple of days. But it all happened so quickly in the end.'

'I'm leaving right now. I'll just have to arrange a couple of things. I'll be there as soon as I can.'

'If you could, he'd appreciate it, I know. It's the Epworth Hospital.'

On the drive to the hospital, the autumn sun is slowly filling the sky with its first pale, cold light. As minutes pass and the horizon brightens, I look at the time on the clock and think about the last minutes of a life which is ebbing away. I find myself stuck on the new freeway. It never seems to end, stream after stream of traffic flowing and merging and separating from every side of the busy underpass. I pass a sign and realise it is my exit, but I cannot change lanes fast enough, and I am swept past the off-ramp, searching in a panic for another way off this choked artery. I find myself ground to a halt behind lines of traffic. I think about the silence and the white snow around me on the skiing trip with John and the girls, and his quiet companionship. I remember the headache and the thoughts which plagued me. I remember John mentioning his illness, and how I was sure he would survive, as he had so often in the past.

I saw John again just after his operation. He was uncomfortable but still vital. We talked for a long time, the constraint of illness and fear dissolved in the easy familiarity of mutual interests. It was late in the afternoon. The birds feasting on the large plum tree outside were making a frenzied twittering—our conversation was almost drowned out by their shrill squeaks. I got up and looked out of the window, and the tree was almost alive with the beating of wings and the beaks plundering the fruit. I described the scene to John while he sat in his chair, and at that moment the twittering of the birds reached a sudden crescendo. A mass of feathered creatures rose in unison from one branch and settled back on another. I looked at John, and we both laughed at the same moment in disbelief at the noise produced by such tiny, inconsequential creatures. I looked at him, and for that moment he looked well again. But later, as we talked, I saw the illness in his face again, like a curtain drawn back over a window. I had seen that look before, but I could not remember where.

Suddenly the Epworth Hospital, a tall, brown-bricked building, rises in front of me. As I search for a space in the crowded parking lot I notice the white knuckles of my hands gripping the wheel tightly. My shoulders feel constricted. Jumping out of the car and hurrying through the glass doors, I hardly notice what I am doing. At the desk I ask impatiently for directions. I am worried about reaching the hospital bed in time. In the lift, I think, 'No, it will be fine. These things invariably take hours, days.'

The doors open on the second floor, and take an age to close again. The doors open and close on the third floor. I prepare myself for the sickbed, the family. I wonder whether John will be conscious, whether he will recognise my face. The door opens on the fourth floor. There is a bustle of nurses and orderlies in the corridor. I walk along and find the ward. Inside, I can see Sonia and John's family near the bed. Sonia is crying, and others look pale, shocked. I stop one of the nurses.

'Has something happened?' I ask. 'I came to see John Weisman.'

'I'm sorry,' she says, simply. 'He died just a few minutes ago. Are you family?'

I look past her at the white bed in the corner, surrounded by heavy banks of intensive-care equipment: screens, blinking lights, drips. And on the bed, hardly disturbing the white smoothness of the sheet, is a pale shape that was my friend.

'No,' I say. 'I'll leave them alone for a while.'

I wait in the corridor, the fluorescent lights buzzing faintly above my head. A traffic light. A parking space. The doors of the elevator opening and closing. And some time in that space, he died. The buzzing of the lights is giving me a headache.

After some time, the nurse puts her head around the door and smiles.

'You can go in now, if you like,' she says.

I walk into the quiet ward and over to the bed in the corner. The shape on the bed is my friend John. I remember his laugh at the sound of the birds in the backyard. I remember the strangely familiar look of illness. And I see that he is gone. I take his warm hand in my own and stand there for some time. I can't avoid thinking of another time when I stood like this, holding the hand of that cold Jonah, my father.

I have taken the whole day off. I return home and leave a message on Sonia's answering machine, offering whatever assistance I can give. I look around the house, unused to being in the house alone on a weekday morning. Then I remember the book, and pull down the lever-arch binder in which I've collected all my research. I look through my documents, interviews, and memos, and I notice a few loose pages at the back. They are the Polish letters my mother gave me months ago. I still haven't had them translated. Now is a good time, I think. I look at the first page.

At the top of the first letter is the imprint of a stamp:

ARTICLES TRICOT ET BONNETERIE

'BOTRICOT'

25, Rue Au Maire, Paris 3e

Tel. ARC. 15-28

The date, too, can be read: 4 Decembre, 1956. And at the bottom it is signed 'R. Marin'.

I look on the next page. It is Ruth Marin, the wife of Julian, Pinkus's younger brother.

I call Krystyna and ask her if she can do a translation. I courier the letters over to her. As soon as she has read them, she calls me. I am almost as dumb-founded as my father must have been on the day in 1956 when he read this letter, which had come from a world he thought had gone forever. I wait impatiently, and as soon as the translations are finished I get them picked up. The first letter is dated 1956, almost exactly ten years after my father returned from Borneo.

Articles Tricot et Bonneterie

'Botricot'

25, Rue Au Maire, Paris 3e

Tel. ARC. 15-28

Paris, 4 December 1956

Dear Mrs Gerber

By coincidence, I met a lady who came from Melbourne whose name I cannot unfortunately remember. She was asking about the children of Pinkus Marin and about the Gerberbaum family. She gave me your address as you are the person who can tell me about Beniek, Stasiek and Guta Marin.

I am Ruth Marin, the widow of, dear to his memory, Julian Marin. You might also remember me, as your name is familiar to me. I would like very much to contact them by letter, hoping you know of their addresses, I am kindly asking you to let them know of my existence in Paris.

I am hoping you would be able to help me find them, as their fate is of great interest to me.

I would be happy if any of them, especially Beniek, immediately wrote to me at the address of the mentioned company, where I can be found,

Kind regards and greetings to you.
R. Marin.

Nellie has told me about the French girl who came to Warsaw as the new bride of Julian Marin, Pinkus's younger brother. I remember Nellie's story of riding through the streets of Warsaw on the *dorozka*, on the way to the opera. So this is my father's aunt—the only other person left alive from the whole family. I believed that the whole family was lost in the shadows of the Holocaust. And now, a decade later, this woman appears, impossibly, out of the past. I wonder what my father must have felt when this letter came—excitement, relief, hope? I can feel my heart thumping loudly as I read the second letter.

Paris, 20 January 1957

My Dear, Dear Stasiek

I held my breath and my hands trembled when I was opening your letter. I was looking for you for so many years. If it wasn't for the hand of fate (coincidental meeting with this unknown lady) I would still not have known anything about you. I thank you very much, my dear boy, that you have written to me immediately. I call you 'my dear boy' because that is how I remembered you. I recall your departure, when we came with, dear is his memory, Julian, to farewell you. Twenty years have passed. You are already a father of two sons and I am older as well, by twenty years, or maybe forty, after all I lived through.

The year 1939: the unforgettable evening of the 6th of September, when all men, just before the German offensive, were leaving Warsaw. It was 11pm when Beniek phoned my dear Julian to ask him to go with him and the others but Julian didn't want to part with me. I heard later that Beniek, and Gutka (she later married) were in Vilnius and that they were later able to get through to you. The news of you not knowing anything about them caused me pain. At present, repatriations are happening all the time—Polish citizens who remained in Russia are returning. I wrote to Warsaw immediately, asking for the whereabouts of Beniek and Gutka. They may have been in Russia all the time! Your father's house at Mila Street, as well as the whole Jewish quarter, do not exist. Everything lies in ruins. We lived through this whole Nazi Gehenna in Warsaw. Later, we were all sent to the camps, where my beloved Julian died in 1943. Destiny decreed that I should survive. My life under the occupation and after the war was very hard. From the moment I lost Julian, my path was strewn with tears. Julian cannot be replaced by anyone in my life—painful memories.

My loneliness was frightening. I could not remain in Poland but had no way out—many women married just to escape this 'second hell.' I also decided to take this step, to try to find my path and in order to be able to exist. I left for Israel, but it was a foreign country, with strange people, and a heavy climate, and I fell ill. The man I married was evil and despotic. During that time, I always thought of the one I had lost, whose memory will always stay with me, and those people dear to him and therefore dear to me.

That's why I was looking for you. I remembered how much he loved the three of you, and I started to think how to escape, how to leave Israel. At last I arrived in Paris, the city where I spent the most wonderful years of my life with Julian. I have had bad luck here, putting all I had into a knitwear business, and still left with nothing.

Your cordiality in writing to me moved me to tears. I can see the Marin character in you. I am sending you a small photograph of Julian, found at a friend's place in Paris. I would like you to have it. I impatiently await your letter and photos.

With regards to you and your family
Your Aunt Ruth

P.S. Stasiek, my dear, while awaiting finalisation of the divorce I use the other surname. In Paris, no-one knows me as anything but Mme Marin (a name so dear to me)

If you want to write to me at my home address, write to Mme Rachgold (this is my surname in all documents)

3 Bov A. Cherioux

Issy-le-Maulineaux (Seine)

France

This tone of trembling excitement is in stark contrast to the tone of the next letter:

Paris, 1 February 1957

Dear Stan,

Although you didn't answer my last letter posted almost a month ago (which surprises me very much) I am writing today, as it is the French and Jewish custom to send holiday greetings. You'll probably receive my letter a few days before Easter, I am sending the Easter greetings to all of you my dears: Stan, Ann and the children.

My warm regards
Ruth

P.S. I will not write anything about myself until I receive your letter. I heard from Warsaw that the Marins were not in the group that recently arrived there. New repatriates arrive every month. I'll let you know immediately if I hear any happy news.

The next letter acknowledges receipt of a cheque, but it was wrongly made out to Ruth Marin, not Ruth Rachgold, which was the surname in her passport. Unable to cash it, she has returned it. She continues:

Your letter was delivered to me yesterday. I've been sick for two weeks. It gives me great joy to look at your family picture, I cannot stop looking at it. I would not recognise you, Stasiek my dear. I remember you as a boy, and now you are a man, with a kind face and a 'Marinowski' smile. Your boys are delightful, and Ann looks very nice. She gave me a great deal of pleasure by writing these few words.

The situation in which I find myself worries and depresses me. As a foreigner I cannot obtain any work here, as I do not have a work permit. I am puzzling over this. My only hope is to apply for compensation from the Germans. They are paying money to the Jews who were in the ghettos, for their moral suffering and imprisonment, for having to wear the star identifying Jews. My papers are already with the German authorities and I am hoping to receive some money in the next few months.

I give you my warmest thanks, anyway, for being interested in my situation and for your kind gesture. God help you. I am very sorry I cannot use the 25 pounds now. You'll know now, that for government authorities and banks you need to write for Ruth Rachgold. You can address letters to R Marin (the surname dear to me).

Many thanks again
Greetings and kisses to everyone
Your Ruth

P.S. Why didn't you mention the photographs I sent you? Did you recognise me? Were you happy to receive your uncle Julian's photograph?

The cheque must have been adjusted and returned to her, because in her next letter Ruth expresses her gratitude:

Paris 2 March 1957

My Dear,

For a whole week I have been in possession of your letter and cheque. Thank you very much. It isn't my custom to delay an answer, but your letter, unfortunately, arrived at the time of my illness. Yes, I agree with you, health is the most important thing in one's life and it is sad when it starts failing.

Your good intentions and willingness to help are really moving. Only yesterday I went to the bank to withdraw 25,000 francs. You ask me what this amount is worth in Paris. A labourer earns 40,000 francs a month; life here is very expensive. For example, I pay 12,000 francs for a small room near Paris. For the most modest living one has to spend 500 francs a day, apart from other expenses. Up until now, I was earning my modest living. As I mentioned in my letter, my only hope is in receiving German compensation. I have already been notified that my case has been approved, it has to go through some other authorities, and this can take a few months. I have to survive this time and wait patiently.

I received a letter from Warsaw where, unfortunately, my elder brother, a doctor, stayed. I was informed that various camps and authorities were written to regarding Beniek and Gutka. I'll let you know if I hear any news. You do not write much, this time. I have nothing against you writing in English—I have difficulty speaking, but fully understand the writing. I thank you very much when a letter from you comes. I would be very happy to see you and kiss you. I hope you will not, Stan, delay your answer. As you see, I wrote this letter a few days ago. Today is a beautiful sunny day, I'll go out to post this letter at the post office. I send the warmest greetings and lots of kisses to you, Ann and the dear children.

Ruth

That is the last letter. Ruth complains that his last few replies have been short and uncommunicative. It is clear from Ruth's words in the last letter that my mother had written instead of my father. Then the letters stopped altogether. My father did not write again. When I finish reading the last letter, I am aghast. It takes me a long time to register that my father really received these letters, and simply stopped writing to this woman. My first thought is disappointment—Ruth might have been able to tell us something about what happened to the family—then shock. I can't believe he just abandoned her. The afternoon is full of meetings, and I don't have any time to think about this. It is only on the way home that it hits me. Surely it can't be true. Something must have happened. I stop the car on the side of the road, and look at the letters again. No, it's very clear:

> You didn't answer my last letter posted almost a month ago (which surprises me very much)

And again, in the last letter:

> You do not write much, this time.

I can feel that sick feeling again, the feeling I had as a child every time my father said to me, 'I can't make it,' or 'I have to work.' I feel the same dread I felt when he stared at me, red in the face, across the table the day I received my conscription letter. I feel the slap across the face that I felt when he said 'They'd never pick a Jew.' What a bastard.

'You're very quiet,' Wendy says.
'Not really,' I say. Then, 'Well, it's been a weird day.' I tell her about the hospital, and then about Ruth, and my father.
'It doesn't make any difference, surely, after all this time?' she says.
'Yes, it does. It makes all the difference. I really thought I had my father worked out. The war, the Holocaust—I thought it explained everything. But it's just beginning to dawn on me that maybe, when all is said and done, he was just a cold, selfish man. Maybe it wasn't anything to do with the Holocaust. Maybe it was just him.'
'What difference does it make now?' Wendy says. 'I'm sure

he loved you in his own way. Or maybe he just wasn't emotional, as you say. Either way, there's no point in obsessing over it now.'

'You know,' I say, 'it could be a family thing. His mother was a Fogel, and the Fogels are just like that. Closed up.'

'Wasn't your mother a Fogel, too?' Wendy asks. I shrug.

'Yes.'

Then, at bedtime she says, suddenly, 'After all, you don't have your father's letters to this woman.'

'No.'

'So maybe you shouldn't take it too seriously. You don't know what really happened. For instance, how could he know for sure it was really her?'

'But he didn't even try to find out. That's what proves it. He just never made an effort.'

'Well,' Wendy says, 'maybe he had his reasons.'

'I'm tired of thinking about it,' I say.

'So what happened to your book?' Dr Goldman says.

'It's a waste of time,' I say. 'I really tried with this grieving thing. I decided I needed to find out something about my father first. But now I can see that he was just a dysfunctional, weak, selfish coward. So what's the point?'

Dr Goldman is impassive, as usual.

'There is a line I have to draw. It's obvious that I'm searching for something that isn't there. I started this because of the headaches. And they're gone now, thanks to you. So that's it. And, after all, I have other responsibilities. So maybe I should just give up.'

Dr Goldman looks at me, his head bent to the side. After a while he says, 'Is that what you want to do?'

'Yes,' I say.

I think about it for a while.

'My dad gets these letters out of the blue—the only person left from his entire family, and he just turns his back on her. I can't understand it. It's not normal, no matter what he'd been through.'

'And why do you think he would do that?'

'I don't know. It's just typical of him. He couldn't care less, in the end. He would much rather ignore it and not have to deal with it. Like everything else.'

'You seem very angry,' he says.

He's right. I can feel my face getting hot. I feel flushed.

'No, I'm not angry,' I say. 'Okay, maybe I am. I just can't see how he could do that, how he could turn away like that. Didn't he give a shit about anyone but himself? God, as if I didn't know that already.'

'I see. You knew it already.'

'Of course,' I say. 'But it still amazes me how disappointed I am, every time. I feel sorry for her, for Ruth. In the letters she just seems so desperate and lonely. Okay, I guess she was asking for money, too. Maybe it was even a scam, I don't know. But I bet he didn't even try to find out.'

'What makes you say that?'

'I've told you … that's what he was like. Just like he never tried to find out if I was unhappy either. He didn't care. As long as he had things the way he wanted, he didn't bother. He just took and took, and gave nothing in return. I had to support him. The way she wrote in the last letters—hurt, alone … it's terrible.'

The doctor stays quiet again, watching me.

'She must have felt … grief. Sitting alone in a rented room in Paris, with no money, no-one to help her. And then the excitement of finding her nephew, a family, a lifeline. She must have felt reborn, like everything was going to be all right. You can tell that from her letters. And then … nothing.'

The doctor closes his eyes and opens them again, as he has a habit of doing.

We sit in silence for a long time. I start thinking about other things. I watch the clock hands turning on the wall. Tick tick tick. Then the time is up.

At John's funeral, I look around at the enormous crowd that has gathered, a sea of people—John's family, his children and their spouses, his grandchildren, dignitaries, friends. It's a warm autumn afternoon, and the cemetery is covered with great maple leaves which drift down from time to time and land with a dry rustling on the carpet of leaves below. At the Chevra Kadisha, his close friends, mostly prominent members of the community, had given speeches and dabbed at their eyes. Now I am adrift among all these people, strangely unified in their memory of a single human life.

I watch Sonia and her family weeping quietly beside the grave. At the last moment, each walks in turn and drops a handful of earth on to the grave. Then Sonia looks across, and motions to me to do the same. I dig my hands into the pile of loose soil, with its faint metallic smell, and pour it through my fingers on to the grave. Then I walk towards the family and try to express my condolences. As I do so, I can feel something inside me, a spasm clutching at my diaphragm. I walk away quickly, the sobs shaking my whole body violently, as though the organism is trying to vomit something out. I put my head in my hands, and cry uncontrollably for a long time. Suddenly I feel a hand on my arm, and the mother of a friend turns me around and puts my head on her shoulder. She is a foot shorter than me, and I am aware that the scene seems a little comic, like a scene in a Marx Brothers film. I start to laugh at this ridiculous picture, bent over in this undignified posture, but I am crying at the same time. After a while I stop shaking, and stand upright. She puts her hand to my cheek and walks away, following the line of mourners. I follow them a little way, too, then I wander off amongst the graves.

I find myself on a small bridge that crosses over a stream running through the middle of the graveyard. I stand there, leaning on the railing and watching the water carrying the leaves and twigs onwards, pushing them through the narrow banks, over the few small stones, and on down the hill, towards the river.

That look I saw on John's face, that curtain of illness which swung back for a moment, then closed again ... I realise that I knew that look from a thousand days with my father. His illnesses, which began as far back as I can remember—the heart attacks, the strokes—were the dominating feature of his life. But, unlike John, he never really struggled against the isolation which illness brought him. He retreated into the illness. It was an excuse, a relief.

And that pathetic voice which I heard in Ruth's letters, that is my voice. I am the one who felt abandoned in a foreign country, waiting for a sign that never came. My father took his silence with him; he never explained any of his life to me. I watch the stream carrying the broken twigs endlessly downhill towards the river. I have found my father's childhood. I have found his departure and arrival. I have found his struggle and his loss. But I have to admit that I have not found my father. The child who cried over his crystal radio set, the boy sailing through the Suez Canal, the soldier who watched his friend bleed to death in the jungle, the man who stopped writing to Ruth, and the Jonah who lay on the hospital bed—all of these are the one person. My father.

Ruth

'Ruth?' my mother says. 'There's nothing to know. Goodness, don't you have anything else to worry about?' She holds her head very slightly bent to one side, her shoulders drawn up in a familiar posture of self-protection.

'She stopped writing to us,' she says. 'That's all that happened. We wrote to her, but she stopped writing.'

'That can't be true,' I say. 'I've read the letters.'

'Oh, can't you let your father rest in peace? He tried his best for you. I know you think he wasn't a good father. I don't understand it. Why can't you just be happy? You have a good job, you have Wendy, and Amy and Rachel.'

'Well, for a start I'm trying to write a book. It's for the girls, later on. But I'm getting stuck at the same point. Everything I've found out so far, the family, the war—it just doesn't explain what really happened to Dad. Why he was the way he was.'

My mother looks pained.

'What do you mean? I don't understand.'

'He was just a kid and he travelled halfway across the world by himself. He managed to survive the war, and losing his family. He must have been a strong person to get through that. So why was it that, after all that, he was incapable of being a father? After everything I've found out, I just can't recognise that man as the person I grew up with.'

'He was sick, you know that. He always had to struggle. Even when he was sick, he still had to support you. You should be grateful to him. He never liked to show how sick he was.' She has the glint of a tear in her eye.

'Oh, come on,' I say, impatiently. 'That's the only thing he ever did show. He hid behind the illness all the time. He gave up long before he got sick. Being sick just gave him an excuse to opt out.'

'You don't know, you don't know,' my mother says, shaking her head sorrowfully. 'Why do you have to be like this?'

'Why do *you* have to be like this?' I say. 'Tell me something, honestly. Why on earth did you marry him?'

She glares at me, shocked. I stare back. She shakes her head, impatiently, trying to avoid the question. I just wait for her to answer.

'He was a good man, a nice man,' she says. 'That's all I can say. The first time I saw him again—that day, at the wharf, leaning against the fence—even then I wanted to marry him.' She shrugs. 'I went out with other boys while he was away. But none of them were like him. He had this something, this confidence. He had a sense of adventure. I loved it. And he ... well, he wanted to settle down after the war. It was only natural, after everything he had been through. He proposed to me five days after he came home. I wanted to say yes straight away, but I waited for a few days—you were supposed to in those days.'

'So what happened to his sense of adventure, his confidence? Did he have a breakdown?'

'I don't know, Bernard. I think you're exaggerating. Yes, he changed, that's true. But there were so many things—the war, his family, his father. He really tried. I can tell you that he tried to be a good father. He just wasn't the kind to make a fuss.'

'Make a fuss?' I shake my head in disbelief. 'That's a bit of an understatement. He never made any sign that he cared at all. Maybe he couldn't care less about any of us. Maybe *that's* the kind of person he was.'

There is a silence. She looks away.

'You don't understand,' she says.

'No,' I say. 'You're right. I don't understand.'

We sit in silence for a while. She seems to be thinking.

'Come with me,' she says, getting up with an exaggerated effort.

I follow her. She walks as though she hardly has the strength for it. I can tell that she is hoping I will relent guiltily at the suffering I am causing her.

She rifles through boxes, sighing audibly at this disorder that my inexplicable curiosity has created.

'Goodness,' she says, 'you certainly do make demands.'

At last she finds what she is looking for—a box of papers and photographs. She sorts through the contents, and hands me a picture in a pewter frame. I can see Dad, dressed as a jockey, and another man; they are arm in arm, with drunken grins spread across their faces. In the background a big party is taking place.

'He wasn't always the way you think, Bernard. It was only later he got that way, when he was sick. You don't remember.'

I stare at the picture for a while. I can hardly recognise this happy, excited, confident man as my father.

'Who's the other guy?' I ask.

'His name is Reuben Solomon. That's all I wanted to show you,' she says. She takes the frame from me abruptly, and starts putting the things back in the box.

Nellie

'Leave me alone, Bernard. I'm dying,' Nellie says. Her breath is coming in short gasps, and she really does look pretty bad.

'Sorry, Nellie, I shouldn't have come,' I say, reluctantly. 'Do you want me to go?' I stand up.

Her breathing seems to improve suddenly.

'Well, you're here now, aren't you? What are you bothering me about this time?'

'No, no,' I say, walking towards the door. 'You're right. I'll leave you to rest.'

Nellie turns away for a moment. Then she turns back irritably.

'Come on, then,' she snaps. 'Don't stand there like an idiot. What do you want to know?' I sit down again, next to the bed.

'All right,' I say. 'I want to know about Ruth.'

'I've told you all I know. I only met her once.'

'No, after the war. Your mother got a letter from her.'

'Well?'

'I want to know about my father. Why he stopped writing.'

'Oh,' Nellie says. 'I don't know anything about that.' She lies there in silence for a while.

'I don't know why you have to bother a dying woman about it,' she wheezes. Then she pushes herself up in the bed energetically.

'I can't tell you anything, anyway. Your father was different when he came back from the war. He had all the softness knocked out of him. He had a wild streak. And it was a bit like that, those years just after the war. I think maybe it was relief at having made it through. And also trying not to think too much about the others, the ones who were gone.

'But I didn't see too much of Stan in that time. I was married already, living in Sydney. It's my sister who told me this. When he came back from the war, before he married your mother, he was living together with my mum and dad and my sister Mary in the house in Elwood. You should go and bother her instead.'

'I'll go and see her,' I say. Nellie nods.

'Now leave me to die in peace,' she says. I get up to leave.

'There's a box of papers at Mary's,' she says. 'A red tin box. You can bring it to me when you've talked to her. If I'm still here.'

'Well ...' Mary says, and she pauses for a while to reflect. 'I suppose you could say that Stan did come back a little bit different.' She pauses, then says quickly, 'But then, I think they all did, all the soldiers. He was always just Stan to me, of course. Like a big brother. We always got along like a house on fire. He was a lovely man.'

I feel very comfortable sitting next to Mary on the sofa. She is one of the few people I remember from my childhood who was able to express any kind of affection. When I tell her about my struggle to understand my father, she takes my hand in hers for a moment. She has tears in her eyes. She tries to assure me that my father was a good man, a good father who loved his family. I would like to believe her. But I remember the letters I have in my pocket.

'What do you mean by "different," exactly?' I ask. She pats my hand and gets up.

'I'll just get us some tea,' she says, and bustles around. When she sits down again, I try again. 'You said he was "'different?"'

'Oh, I don't know, really,' she says. 'It's hard to say. This will sound a bit silly, but I just remember that before the war he used to poke me and tickle me, like an older brother does to a little sister. He was quiet, reserved, warm, still very much from the old world. But when he came back, he wasn't like that any more. He was a man, much more grown up. I suppose it was the war, as much as other things.'

'Well,' I say, bitterly. 'Maybe that's just what he was like when he grew up. People change.'

'Well, no, I think there were other things.'

'You know,' I say, 'when you look at it, it's hard to avoid the conclusion that he was just an emotional cripple. We all skirt around it. Whenever I ask, everyone says what a lovely man he was. Even you. But, let's face it, he was a crappy father. And now I can see that he was a pretty crappy human being.' I take the letters from my pocket and read them to her. She sits in silence for a while.

'There was something else,' Mary says. 'When his father died. Just before the war. You knew that?'

'Yes,' I say. 'But I don't know very much. No-one ever seems to mention it. How did he die?'

'Well, of course, I can't tell you much,' she says quickly.

'I'm surprised Nellie didn't mention it,' I say.

'Well,' Mary says. 'She was in Sydney that whole time.'

'So when exactly did it happen?' I ask.

'Oh, not long after Stan arrived here. I must have been seven or eight.'

'I guess he was upset.'

'He was devastated. He couldn't go back to Warsaw for the funeral, of course. And he hardly even had any contact with his family. And when he came back from the war he was different, like I said.' She gets up from her chair. 'Frank can tell you. Frank?' She calls her husband from the other room.

'Bernard wants to know about Stan,' Mary says. 'When he came back from the war. Do you remember?'

'Bit of a larrikin, wasn't he?' Frank says.

'Yes,' Mary says, and laughs. 'Oh, yes. I remember the time he came home on leave and drank eight beers in a row at our house. He was careering all over the place, giving me five-pound notes out of his wallet, and laughing and knocking things over in the hall. My mother got so angry that she chased him out of the house with a broom. You remember how tiny Mum was, and there she was, running down the street after this soldier in his khakis, shouting at him in Polish.'

'Did he still speak Polish?' I ask.

'Oh no, not at all. By that time he was a real Australian. A digger. You would hardly tell him from the other soldiers apart from his name, and his accent. And anyway, he had started calling himself Stan. He swore quite a lot, too.'

'No, that was later,' Frank interjects.

'Well,' says Mary, 'he already had some pretty colourful language when he came home from the war. He'd get a bit peeved with my mother, because he said she nagged him all the time about his drinking, smoking, swearing. In the end they had a bit of a showdown, and he moved out.'

'I've never seen anyone try so hard to fit in,' Frank says. 'He tried too hard. I think having a bunch of mates during the war gave him something he'd never had. A lot of them were like that. He hated the war itself, the killing and so on. But when he came back, there was something missing. Melbourne must have been pretty small change after all that.'

'No, no,' Mary interrupts. 'I don't think so. He was really a loving man. Maybe it was hard to see sometimes, but I could tell; if you knew him really well, you could tell. It's just … there were things …' Mary stops, and looks at Frank.

'For one thing, he was too much under Reuben's influence.' Frank says. 'Or maybe it was the other way around. They were always about together, him and Reuben, up to one thing or another. Stan would have done a lot better if he could have set his mind to one thing, instead of latching on to Reuben like that. But he was too easily swayed. It was Reuben who brought out the swearing and the drinking; they got into the gambling and all sorts of other rackets. I suppose he was looking for some of the excitement of the war again. He was an S.P. bookie for a few years—did you know that? And he had a couple of racehorses himself at one time. Part owner, of course. He and Reuben used to run the bookmaking on the wrong side of the law down in St Kilda with Henry Feldman and a few others. I suppose he took after his dad in that. Gambling, it's a dangerous thing …'

Mary jumps up suddenly, cutting him off, and offers me some tea.

'Wouldn't you like something to drink?'

I can see, with long experience of the family, that we've reached the end of the conversation. But when I leave the house, Frank walks me to the car.

'There's one thing I can say,' he says. 'Your dad was an intelligent man, a really smart man, and he had a lot of potential. Everyone could see it. But there were reasons why it never came to anything in the end. The gambling was one. He always kept it under control, but I could see it meant a hell of a lot to him.'

'But why?' I ask.

'I can't say entirely,' Frank says. 'There were lots of reasons. Most of all, I think he missed his dad. I always thought he was trying in his own way to be like him.'

'I'm thinking of going to see Reuben Solomon,' I say.

Frank is quiet for a while. Then he says, 'Yes. Maybe you should do that.'

Brothers

Melbourne, 1956. The city shone like a new bride as the world rolled up on her doorstep, a little weary after the gruelling thirty-six hours' plane ride it had taken to reach her. It was a new city, one which was being transformed by waves of migrants from many lands looking for a place of refuge or a better life. They were changing irrevocably the old British colony on Aboriginal land that had been settled by convicts, squatters, and settlers. Now the first European cafes had begun spilling on to the pavements of Carlton and St Kilda, and culture and sophistication seemed to have blown in like a cloud carried by the war. The city was decorated everywhere for the Games, as the Olympic torch made its way from fist to fist across the continent.

In July, at his house in Toorak, Reuben Solomon held a fancy-dress party for his friends. Like so many couples across the country who had rushed to get married in the euphoria of the war's end, Reuben and his wife Sela were now celebrating their tenth anniversary. Reuben was dressed as Samson, with a tunic and a huge black mane of flowing locks; and Sela was Delilah, sporting a plunging cleavage and wielding a large pair of scissors. At midnight, the lights suddenly went out, and there was dead silence for a few moments. Then the lights flashed on, and a man dressed as a jockey entered the room mounted on a horse. A loudspeaker blared, 'And it's Cheeky Chap, edging ahead on the last bend, yes Cheeky Chap into the straight, followed by Martaz and Florilles, and it's Cheeky Chap, Cheeky Chap for the win.' The party broke into applause, and my father, in a jockey's peaked cap and jodhpurs, climbed down from his precarious perch on top of his two friends who were suffering badly from overheating inside the horse costume. He walked to my mother, who was dressed in the style of the roaring twenties, and proceeded to get roaring drunk.

I am in Reuben's apartment, looking at the square black-and-white photograph of my parents at the party, the companion photo to the one I saw at my mother's house. In the photo, Stan looks happy, with a blissful, confident smile, perhaps a little more self-assured for the beer he has drunk while waiting for his grand entrance. My mother looks nervous, slightly disapproving in her flapper costume. But she will not say anything: she will smile and get him home to sleep it off.

'"Skret!"' Reuben says, coming back into the room with a couple of glasses on a tray. He spits the word out, and glares at me. I stare back at him. I have no idea what he is talking about.

'That was the first thing he said to me. It's Polish. It means "roll-your-own" cigarettes. He saw me smoking a rollie, and he said "Skret!" in this high-and-mighty way. I didn't like him at all at first. I thought he was such a *kvetch*, coming here and acting like Melbourne was a bloody backwater. You know, I'm from Warsaw, too. I just got the hell out of there a lot earlier, that's all.'

I feel a little uncomfortable about coming here. I know that my father and Reuben had a falling-out in the 1960s, and that they never spoke again. Now Reuben is in his eighties, but he still goes to his office every day. He tells me this several times.

'I still go in every day. Only ask Artie Greenvach, he'll tell you. You don't believe me?'

I tell him I believe him.

'Anyway,' he says, 'I met him first at one of these welcome parties they used to have, when new people arrived in Melbourne. Then after that I didn't see him again for a long time. A couple of years later, in the middle of the war—'41, '42—he called me up when he was going to the Middle East, to ask what he was in for. Bit nervous, I suppose. I told him, well, you know, it gets pretty hot round the pyramids.' Reuben chortles to himself. 'After that, when he turned up here on leave, we'd go out and have a few drinks, a bit of a good time. He was not such a bloody *schlemazel* as I thought. No, he was okay.'

'How'd you two get into business together?' I ask.

'Well, a couple of years after the war, he came to me with a proposal: we should buy out my brother Alec's coat-making business. He'd done a bit of work with his uncle in handbags and such, so he could see the opportunity. But, of course, he didn't have a copper nickel to his name. So he needed me to get terms with Alec, and that's what we did. And we made our money back in a couple of years, and sold the business at a profit. All the same, I would never say it, but he had no head for business, your father. Just didn't have the backbone.' Reuben shifts nervously in his chair, and then shrugs and glares at me. He is still very angry, though he tries to disguise it. I know his tone very well, from my own voice. Suddenly I feel the need to defend my father.

'But I thought the coat business was Dad's idea.'

'Oh, well.' Reuben shrugs. He looks away and snorts.

'What I'm saying is,' he continues, 'he relied on me to make the decisions ninety-nine per cent of the time. He was never the mover. He was a good follower, yes, but a businessman?'

'But it was Dad's idea? The coats business?'

He waves his hand dismissively.

'And you stayed in business together for twenty years?'

'We were lucky. But it didn't last.'

'Henry Feldman reckoned that your Chapel Street operation made a lot of money.'

'Well, that wasn't really business, now was it? It was … a little venture on the far side of the law, shall we say. And it damn near ruined us both. Names in the papers, police at the house. Okay, it was fun for a while, and we made a fair bit of money, but you have to know when to walk away. The sandwich bar—now that was a proper business, and we made not too bad a profit on it, too. Bought another one in La Trobe Street in the city. Sold that and started a construction business. And then the nurseries. You must have been old enough to remember them. They were really a big mistake.'

'And it was around then that this picture was taken? Your tenth anniversary?'

'Your dad got blind drunk. He was wetting the heads of his racehorses, he reckoned. He was flying high.'

Reuben seems very bitter. I realise we could go on with this game for a long time. So I cut to the chase.

'Tell me what happened, Reuben.'

'What do you mean?' Reuben says, taken aback. 'I don't know what you mean.'

'Look at him here. He's a happy guy. Maybe he's drunk but, as you said, he was flying high. And that's how I remember him, in the nursery, when I was a little kid. But later he changed. He wasn't like that any more. So when did the fall come?'

I watch Reuben's face change, soften a little for a moment. He seems about to say something. Then he moves uncomfortably in his chair.

'You didn't let me finish my story. Financially, the nurseries were a disaster. It didn't take us two years to cut our losses and sell up. We got back into building, and hooked up with Colt & Co. Real Estate in Ripponlea for a couple of years. Then we set up on our own in Jules Meltzer's building. Rent free. I guess Jules took pity on your dad. The building company wasn't solvent, so in the end we had to close that, too.'

'What went wrong?'

'Let's leave that alone. I don't want to dig up the past. You want to know the story, and I'm telling you. It was then that Artie Greenvach offered me a partnership, and I brought Stan in, too, out of friendship, because we'd always done everything together. It was a good deal—lots of potential to build up the business. But it was never enough for Stan. And it was starting to be an embarrassment for me in front of Artie. I'd been carrying your dad for years, and it was time to stop. He couldn't make a decision for himself. He always had to rely on me. And he wasn't interested in real estate—he used to sit in the office all day and read the *Racing Guide* …'

Reuben is getting heated again.

'So he didn't take to business,' I say.

'Business?' he says, snorting. 'No. That wasn't his style. You know, one day when we were out, I saw your dad tossing a coin with some guy. The fella said, "What's the stake? Hundred quid?" Stan said, "Make it five hundred." It was stupid, I knew he didn't have money like that. I could see his eyes glittering. They chucked up the coin. Stan called heads. He won the first toss. Then the other guy said, "Double or nothing?" and Stan said, "Sure". A second toss, and it was heads again, and now your dad was up £1000. They bet again—and Stan won. They kept doubling the ante, and doubling again, until Stan was richer by £32,000. It was a goddamn fortune. But Stan wouldn't stop. He called heads again. The coin went up and came down tails. They shook hands and walked away. He lost £32,000. I would have gone in and talked to him. But then I got a look at his face, and for once he looked happy.'

Reuben is quiet for a moment. He strums his fingers on the table.

'By that time, I'd already decided I wanted out. I went and spoke to your mum. She always had a lot more sense than he did. I said, we both know something's wrong with Stan. He's a great guy, I said. You know he's always helping other people. Now he needs to help himself. Sela and I will buy him out.'

He looks at me angrily, then throws up his hands.

'Business is business. There's only so far you can go. I made him a fair offer. One of us has got to buy the other out, fair's fair. All right, I knew he wasn't in a position to buy me out. So that made it easier for him, didn't it? It was me who was taking the risk, putting money down on the table. And he agreed, didn't make a fuss, just shook hands, and that was that. But then, at the last minute, he kept queering the deal. It was just like him. First it wasn't enough money.

So I agreed to up the price by ten per cent. Then he insisted all the negotiations had to go through Jack Rosenfeld, our accountant. I agreed to that, too. Then, finally, on the day we were going to sign, he rang me and said, since it was on terms, he wanted Sela to guarantee the sale. That was the last bloody straw. I agreed but, after that, never a word passed between us again.'

Reuben stops. He looks like he's going to get up, then he slumps back in the chair. He looks all of his eighty years.

'I'm still in the real estate business, you know. And I go into the office every day,' he says. 'Just ask Artie Greenvach.'

On the way back home, I get a call from Mary Klepner.

'Nellie called me about this red box,' she says. 'Apparently you were supposed to pick it up.'

'Oh hell,' I say. 'I forgot. I'll drop by and get it now.'

I stop at Mary and Frank's house, and have a cup of tea. I tell them about Henry Feldman and Reuben Solomon.

'Yes,' Frank says. 'It was quite a world your dad was involved in then.'

'It was the happiest time of his life,' I say. 'Why did he give it up?' Mary and Frank look at each other.

'Well, maybe it was just time,' Mary says, after a moment. She gets up.

'I'll get that box down for you. I don't know why Nellie was so insistent on you bringing it over.'

The next day is a Saturday, and I go to see Nellie at the Montefiore.

'Did you bring that box?' she says. 'You certainly took your time. I had to ring Mary about it.'

'Sorry,' I say. I hand her the box.

'It's only for you that I was getting it, you know. Since you're always bothering me.' She snorts, and opens the box. It is full of old papers and photographs. She takes out a small, worn sheet of writing paper, once folded in four. Some of the writing is difficult to read, where the paper is worn along the creases.

'To my dear uncles and aunt,' one of the pages says, in careful schoolboy copperplate:

> Many thanks for your letter and for the pound you sent me. I am very glad you remember me. How are you? How is business? I should like to see you. I hope that when I finish my school that I go to Australia to be with you and with uncle Nathan. How is he? Tell him that his daughter is a young Miss. This week she is four years. We all are well. Please write to us every week. Our best regards and kisses to you.
> Yours Beniek.

I read the letter over a number of times in silence. This careful writing is the last trace of Beniek, my uncle. My father's older brother. This letter is written long before my father left Warsaw. The young miss is my mother, Nathan's daughter, living with Pinkus and Sara in Ogrodowa Street, before times changed.

It is a very long moment before I look up into Nellie's eyes. They are filled with tears. She blinks them back angrily.

'You see this?' she says, simply. 'You need to understand this. Your father loved Beniek, he loved him very much. It was Beniek who wanted to come to Melbourne after me, when he finished school. My father was going to organise a permit for him. I remember him at the station when I left. He was so excited. He promised to see me again, to come and make a great success in Australia.'

'But why didn't he?'

'I don't know. Not for certain,' Nellie says. 'Maybe he changed his mind. It was a terrible time. It was 1937, things were getting very bad. Life was hard for everyone, and for Jews it was worse.

Pinkus lost a lot of money, they lost their beautiful apartment. I heard something that Beniek didn't want to leave his friends behind. And my father had only one permit. Anyway, I think maybe he was eldest, so he felt he should stay and look after the family. And he sent his little brother instead.'

'So he saved Dad's life, then, in a way.'

'He didn't know what could come after. But yes, I think maybe it's true.'

'Did you ever talk to Dad about it?'

'To Stan? No, no. He wouldn't talk about it at all. Not even to remember the things from before the war. He would get angry. He didn't speak Polish to me any more, or Yiddish. He didn't want to think about it any more.'

'But it still seems strange to me. If he loved Beniek, how could he just forget about him like that? And then, when Ruth wrote, maybe there was a chance that they could find out something about what happened to him. Maybe he was alive somewhere. Dad never went over to try to find him, or Gutka.

'Well, they would have known he was here, in Melbourne. They had addresses here, my father, my uncle. And there were other reasons, maybe, why he didn't want to find out any more …' Nellie stops.

'Yes, go on. What reasons?'

'No, nothing,' she says. 'I'm sure it was only that. He loved Beniek, and he came out in Beniek's place. There was only one permit.'

She is silent for a minute.

'Couldn't your father have organised another permit?'

She turns her head away.

'It was too late then. Bernard,' she says flatly, 'I'm tired now. I don't want to talk any more. I'm an old lady. I have to sleep.'

'There was only one permit.' My mother repeats Nellie's words. We're in the park, walking, while the children play among the autumn leaves.

'There was a reason Beniek couldn't come. It was hard to get landing permits, and expensive, too—perhaps forty pounds, which was a lot. Jacob got one for Beniek but he wanted to come with his friends. He had so many friends, and he didn't want to come alone. So your father came instead.

'Your father didn't like to talk about it,' she says. 'He never heard from Beniek again after the war. But that was why we chose your name, Bernard. I suggested it, and he agreed. I would have liked to call you Ben, but he didn't want it, and we couldn't be sure he was still alive. He didn't like to talk about it, even to me. The only time I saw how he felt was when his father died, and he came round to our house. He couldn't hold the letter, because his hands were trembling so much. So my father had to read it to him. It said that Pinkus had had a heart attack. And afterwards he came to me and he just cried, for a long time. He never mentioned it again.

'Then, after the war, we went to the Red Cross, hoping they could tell us something about his family. But we heard nothing at all, and after a while we just got on with our lives. Lots of people were in the same position. You just didn't talk about it. So we just went on with things, and then those letters came out of the blue, from Ruth in Paris.'

In the background I can hear the shouts of the girls, chasing each other around among the plane trees.

'You've read the letters. I don't remember them so well now, but I know she thought there might be news of Ben and Gutka. Things were going well for us at the time, and I suppose your father hoped—you know how it is—I suppose he thought that perhaps there was some hope after all.

'But the letters came, and there wasn't any news. I saw the disappointment in his face. And I think he decided that was it, enough. He wouldn't rake it all up again. So he stopped writing. And I couldn't help but be a little bit relieved. But then the troubles started, first with the nurseries, and then a whole string of businesses. He couldn't settle to one thing. And he lost some of the confidence he had after the war. But we made do with what we had, and we tried our best. I know he wasn't the most affectionate person, afterwards. He was so sick, all through those years. But he did try …'

My mother looks at me imploringly. She doesn't have any answers for me. Perhaps she is just as lost and confused as I am. The girls are racing around among the trees.

'Then he was talking to one of the salesmen, and he just collapsed,' my mother is saying. 'He was leaning against a partition. His feet gave way under him, and he just slid down the wall. It was a stroke, the doctors said. It was 1966, just before his break with Reuben. I couldn't believe that Reuben would treat a man that way—a friend—when Stan was so ill. I didn't know how we'd get through it, with you both at school. Stan was terribly worried about me being left with nothing if Reuben failed on his obligations. Even though he would have walked away, he refused Reuben's first offer because it was much too low. And he asked Sela to guarantee the deal—she had money behind her. Reuben was so difficult, he insisted on taking every little thing to the lawyer, and your father was so weak, it was a crime to treat him like that.

'Every day I would go to the hospital, and he'd give me instructions on what to tell the contractors on the building site. Then I'd take the train up, and I'd arrange everything. If we hadn't kept the business going, we couldn't have made it through that time.'

'And he never spoke to Reuben again?'

'No,' Mum says. Her face wanders. 'Well, later he wanted to, but I wouldn't let him. Not after what Reuben had done to him—I couldn't bear to see him go back and make up. I put my foot down. But perhaps I was wrong. I think maybe he needed a family of his own. He needed a brother, and Reuben was the nearest thing.'

I think about the time when he had his first stroke. I was

sixteen. So much was happening in his life, but he never spoke a word about it. Did he think he was saving us from it, or did he just not trust anyone else with his feelings? Or had he simply shut himself off from feeling anything at all? When the stroke came, it almost seems as though those things were reaching back out of the past to strike him down. They never let go their hold—he had a series of strokes and heart attacks over the following years, and then open-heart surgery as well. The organism was shutting down. And finally, in May 1985, he collapsed, playing cards as usual on Friday night. The ambulance took him to Prince Henry's, but by that time the doctors knew he would never recover any degree of consciousness. Paul and I listened to the doctor, and we looked at each other, and for once we knew what our father would feel, what he would want. We asked that he not be kept alive on life support. The next day, he died. I was relieved for him and for myself, too. I just wanted to live my life. But now, standing with my mother among the trees, I feel a wave of frustration rising in me. He took so many things with him forever, leaving me to straggle along this cold trail of facts without anyone to guide me, to search for understanding amongst the scattered debris of his life. I have struggled this far, but I know that something is still missing.

On an impulse, I get the telephone and call my brother.

'Paul,' I say. 'Bernard.'

'Hi, what is it?' he asks. 'I'm really up to my neck here. I can't talk now.'

'Can we meet for lunch?' I say. 'Half past one? Wherever you like.'

'Where we usually meet.'

In the cafe, Paul asks, 'Did you want to talk about something?'

'No,' I say. 'Not really.' It isn't true, but I'm not sure where to start.

'Oh, I heard that you went to see Reuben Solomon.'

'Yes,' I say. 'It was strange. I felt guilty, because of Dad. But I needed to know what happened. They were like brothers, and then …'

'Hmmm,' he says. 'So. What are you ordering?'

'I don't know. I'm not really hungry.'

Paul looks at the menu.

'Did I tell you?' I say. 'John Weisman died last week. I went to the funeral yesterday.'

'Oh, that's really sad,' Paul says. 'He was a really great guy.'

'I went to see him at the Epworth. But I didn't make it in time. I got there a couple of minutes too late.'

'It was strange,' I say. 'It reminded me of Dad.'

Paul shrugs. 'No, Dad died at Prince Henry's.'

'I don't mean when he died, actually. I was thinking about when he had the bypass surgery in 1979.'

'Oh, yeah, I remember. He was pretty bad.'

'You stayed in London, actually. I had to go and cope with him on my own.'

'Well,' Paul says, 'I was going through my own things. And it was probably better that way. I only fought with him anyway. You always seemed to get along with him fine.'

'Well, no,' I say. 'Even if you fought with him, you were closer. I resented having to cope with him on my own. It was like looking after a stranger.'

'I don't see why you say that. He was a lot like you, in many ways.'

'I don't see that at all. I don't have his temper, or his appetite for taking risks.'

'Well, he was a workaholic, for a start. He was always working, even when he was sick. And he was so meticulous. Even with his gambling—he kept perfect records of everything.'

'Well, I don't know about that,' I say. 'Maybe with his gambling. It's the only thing he seemed to have any feeling for. Maybe he was just a cold bastard.'

'No, I don't think that's really true,' Paul says.

'Well I never once remember him saying that he loved me.'

'No, he wasn't the type to say that. But I felt it all the same.'

'I didn't.'

'I always knew he was a wounded man. He was fucked up, all right. I guess we all are. But I can't say he was cold.'

For the first time, I tell him the story about my conscription. I wonder why I haven't talked to him about it before.

'There was once,' my brother says, 'just after I finished school, and I had to think about uni, career, and stuff. It was all too heavy for me, and I looking for some way to opt out. So when the war broke out in Israel in '67, my friend Geoff and I wanted to join up, go over there. As I say, the main reason was that I just wanted to get out of school.' He laughs. 'But I told Dad, and he said, "We'll check it out. Give it a week." And he called Geoff's parents, and organised for someone to come and talk to us about the war. This guy from the embassy came, and we listened. But then, at the end of the talk, Dad just broke down and started crying. He said, "You don't bring up kids to lose them like that." He was really distraught, weeping. I never saw him like that before. And so we decided not to go, after all. Geoff's parents were so relieved, too. They were always grateful to him.'

I have never heard a story like this from my brother before. I am really amazed. We eat in silence for a while. I think about the look on my father's face, at the dinner table, when he thought I might be sent to Vietnam. I think about Dad and his older brother, and his two sons.

'Nellie told me something,' I say. 'Did you know Dad's brother Beniek was supposed to come to Australia instead of him?'

'Beniek?' says Paul. 'Was that his name? Yeah, Max told me something like that once.'

'I was named after him,' I say.

'Oh, really?'

'I haven't sorted out exactly why Dad came to Australia instead of him.'

The waiter is pouring wine into the glasses.

'Oh, I know that,' Paul says. 'Max said the family lost all their money. So the older brother couldn't come. He had to look after the family. He was studying to be an engineer, but he had to work in a fruit shop or something. And then, of course, the father killed himself. So he had to stay there.'

'He killed himself?'

'Yes, that's what I heard. Nobody talks about it, of course. Family secret. You know how Mum is. She keeps tight lipped on things like that.'

'I've never heard you mention it before.'

'I thought you knew.'

Paul has finished eating. He puts down his fork and motions to the waiter.

'I've got to make a move,' he says.

The Last Act

'Mum,' I say, 'how did Pinkus die? I know it wasn't a heart attack. I need to know the truth.'

She sits frozen in the seat for a long time. After a couple of minutes, she slowly turns and looks at the girls messing around in the back seat. She turns back to me.

'SU-I-CIDE,' she mouths silently, so they can't hear.

I look at her face. It is almost relieved. The momentary relaxation lets me see the years of tension and worry that are etched into her face. She looks at me very honestly for a moment. It is a look I have not seen before. Then I notice how she shrinks again a moment later, bracing herself for the onslaught of my questions. Her shoulders hunch with pain. I can see that she is old, tired. I can see how much she loved my father, how much she misses him. I can see how old and how deep this silence is.

'That's all I wanted to know,' I say. 'Thanks.' As we drive on, I glance across, and I see her shoulders relax a little.

'Have a good flight, Mum,' I say when we part.

'Give it four weeks,' Dr Goldman says when I tell him that I've decided to finish my therapy.

'Why four?' I say. 'Why not two? Why not six?'

'It's just a number,' he says. 'It's also the Jewish period of mourning.'

'Okay,' I say. After a while, I say, 'Actually, I admit I'm kind of scared of stopping this. I'm afraid it might all start all over again.'

'Four weeks,' Dr Goldman says.

In the following week I search for some clue which would help me to understand Pinkus's suicide. I look through book after book to find some reference to social conditions in this period just before the war. Was it the changing political situation, the growing fear and hatred, the threat of war, the shadowed future for his family, which led him to despair? Or was it a more personal reason—a raft of gambling debts, a feeling of failure as a husband or a parent, or simple black depression? I feel that odd doubt which hangs about this word, 'suicide', the fear of instability, madness, desperation, which haunts us all. This one word is enough to make it all seem possible.

Finally, in a book I find a brief footnote reference to a text, On the Eve of Destruction, published in Argentina in 1951, with a chapter on suicides. I try the State Library and the National library. They attempt to locate it using international library databases, but they can find no trace. I try to locate it on the internet, and I find myself ringing bookstores all over the world. After a month or so I am completely frustrated, and I ring the State Library again. The librarian listens patiently to my outpouring of anguish, and then asks me if I have contacted the Kadimah library in Elsternwick.

The Kadimah librarian returns to the telephone in two minutes.

'It's right here in my hand,' she says in a broad Yiddish accent. 'You want to come get it?'

'I'll come straight away.'

'But you know it's in Yiddish? You can read it?' My heart sinks.

'No,' I say. 'I can understand a few words, that's all. My parents only spoke Yiddish when they didn't want us to understand what they were saying.'

'So we'll find you a translator. You want the whole book?'

'No, I only need one chapter.'

'Well, maybe Moshe can help a little bit. What a shame, 'nobody's teaching their kids any more to speak Yiddish. Ask for me, Rachelle.'

When I arrive at the library she is much as I pictured her—a woman in her sixties, with a sheitel, and brimming with Yiddishkeit.

When she sees me, she begins shouting for Moshe straight away. He comes bustling over, raising his eyes to me and shaking his head.

'Always with the shouting,' he says. 'You need to read this book?'

'Yes,' I say. 'I'm writing a family history.'

They begin to pore over the book.

'Yes, it is here, the chapter "Suicide,"' Moshe says. 'Beginning page hundred forty-two.'

He begins to translate for me. The chapter begins by declaring that it is not only Jews who were driven to commit suicide and abandon children on the streets, but unemployed Poles also. The author provides an example of a desperate Pole in Lodz who killed his children with an axe and then hanged himself. He describes the terrible hunger and poverty spreading through Poland at this time.

Rachelle argues with him over some of the words, and their rich, musical voices ring through the library. But, as I listen to Moshe slowly translating the second page, I feel my skin begin to prickle:

> And yet there is something about the Jewish suicides that makes them *different*. It could easily be established that Jews committing suicide were not people who were already starving, but those who were afraid

of the *impending* hunger; those who became tired of life, not from long-standing hunger, but from struggling with that devil, that pushes to the abyss, that tears the morsel from your mouth, that exhausts you spiritually for so long, until all your soul-powers are drawn out and you are transformed into a little plaything in the hands of gloomy thoughts and seductive spectacles.

'No,' shouts Rachelle. 'What are you saying? Not spectacles. What is that—eyeglasses? It means ghosts, which haunt you.'

'Spectres, that's what I meant,' says Moshe, rolling his eyes, 'not spectacles.' He continues. 'Gloomy thoughts and seductive spectres.' He nods at Rachelle. She nods back.

'"The Pole who commits suicide because of unemployment is physically exhausted; the latter, the Jewish boss, that hangs himself in his tallis and tefillin in his several-roomed lodging, is spiritually exhausted."'

'You know what are tallis and tefillin?' Rachelle asks.

'I know the tallis,' I say. 'It's the prayer shawl.'

'The tefillin are little boxes,' Rachelle says.

'No, no, not just boxes,' Moshe says. 'They have in them verses from the Torah. They should be strapped to the body during prayer.'

'Yes,' I say, 'I think I know what you mean.'

Moshe continues. '"… the Jewish suicide is a sign of sickness, of tiredness, of hopelessness, of the spiritual exhaustion of a whole class of people, of a group."' He stops. 'It is enough? So we'll get a translator to do the rest of the chapter.'

'It's a terrible thing to read about,' Rachelle says. 'To think that people were killing themselves, and such horrible things just about to happen. If they knew, I think they wouldn't do it. They would stay alive, just to survive. When you live through the worst, you understand how life is important, no matter how bad things are going on. Life, it's the only thing.'

As she speaks, I can hear a different note in her voice. I can tell that she was there, that she saw some of the things she is speaking of.

'I would like to come and talk to you again, sometime,' I say.

'Any time you like,' she says. 'It's a pleasure.'

I go to see Nellie at the nursing home. She is very ill, and I sit near her quietly, trying hard not to blurt out the questions which rise tactlessly to my lips.

'Well,' she says, in a croaky voice. 'What is it you want to know this time?'

'Nothing, Nellie. You just rest. You're very ill.'

'Don't tell me how ill I am,' she says, raising herself slightly from the pillow.

'You're right. I'm sorry,' I say.

'Come on then, what is it?' she says, more softly. 'You can ask what you like.'

'I've been trying to find out about Pinkus's death.'

Nellie looks disconcerted.

'He was never well, the poor man. He had terrible problems. And not surprising, what with gambling, smoking. He used to light one cigarette off the other. We used to say he only used one match a day. So that's why he had always to go to the Dolomites, to Merano, its very beautiful scenery, for the rest cure. Did some business there, too, though, while he was there. He took us all along once. It was so lovely and cool in the mountains.'

'I found a book on suicide at the Kadimah library,' I say. 'It explains a lot about why he did it.'

'Oh,' She stares at her wrinkled hands. 'Well. How did you find out?'

'So you knew already.'

'Sulla Savicki was the one who told me. Perhaps she told your mother, too. Myself, I couldn't bear to talk about it. He was like a father to me. It was a terrible thing.'

'Who is she, Sulla Savicki? Do I know her?'

'She was my cousin on my father's side.'

'She's not still alive?'

'No. It was only when she was dying that she told me. I stayed with her for several nights. One night, it was very late, and all at once she began to talk about all of it, about Warsaw and the ghetto, and Sara and Pinkus. She needed to tell someone all of the things she'd seen. Frightful things. Many of the things I told you about the ghetto—I heard them from her those nights. She knew how much I loved Pinkus, and she wanted to tell me herself, so I wouldn't find out later and judge him very badly. In the late thirties, she said, things were getting worse for the Jews. First there was the depression, then the anti-Semitism, worse and worse, especially after Pilsudski died. It was hard to make a living as a Jew unless you had a lot of money saved behind you.

'It was then I think Pinkus could know how much his gambling had cost him. Little by little he had to sell, first the warehouses, then the block of flats, and the apartment, too. But he couldn't bear to give to his family the truth even then. Sara was buying new clothes and expensive crystal. He sent away to Australia his youngest son, that he loved. Because he knew that he couldn't afford to pay Stan's schooling, Beniek's college, to pay for Gutka's wedding dress, maybe even to pay the butcher—couldn't pay the rent when it was collected in the courtyard where he used to sit as the owner.

'I think he couldn't bear it any longer. It was like that, in those days, before the Germans. People couldn't bear to watch their lives slipping away, losing their social position, letting down their family. So many men just came home one day and killed themselves. Later, Sulla said, in the ghetto, people didn't kill themselves—it was the opposite, everyone wanted to hang on to life just one more day, to see the Germans lose the war before they died. But Pinkus never saw any of that. And if he'd known what he left them behind to face, I know he would never have done it. She said that he hanged himself. But other people said he jumped from a window. In things like that, people don't always tell the details. But the story itself, it was the same.'

'Did Dad know?'

'I never talked about it to him. I remember when he got the news about Pinkus's death, how he cried, and I did the same. But, you know, there wasn't anything he could do to change it—he couldn't go back to help his family, he couldn't ever see his father again. And so many people knew about it, someone must have told him. But we all knew in the family that nobody was to ever talk about it. That's how it was in those days; there were so many things you didn't talk about.

'Then later he got into the trouble for bookmaking. A lot of people were worried, after what happened to Pinkus. I heard that your grandfather, Nathan, had a talk with him. I don't know what it was he said; but, after that, Stan was not a bookmaker any more. He tried the businesses, but he didn't have his heart in it. He liked the gambling—it was like Pinkus at the races, with all the money and the excitement.

'Stan never talked about it. Maybe he was frightened that he would make his father look bad. He wanted to keep the good memory, so he buried all of the other things away inside him. And he felt it, too, that he shouldn't have left his family, that he could have saved Pinkus, and Ben who should have come in his place, and his mother and his sister. We all feel it a little bit, because we left them all behind to that. But him most of all.'

The nurse comes in and motions to me, and I get up to leave, sadly. I have a thousand questions to ask, but none of them will give me the answers I need. As I'm going, Nellie says croakily: 'I couldn't bear it. Nobody wanted it to be true. Even now I don't believe it. He wasn't the type. I wish I could only have spoken to him a little bit.'

There are tears rolling down her old, lined cheeks.

I go outside and walk again around the streets with their nature strips and neat little trees. I, too, wish that I'd had the courage to confront my father with the past before it was too late. There were things locked up in silence which kept us on different continents. I remember my father leaving for his only journey overseas after the war, to visit my brother in Britain. At the airport, I saw tears on his face, but I couldn't ask him why. In London, Paul suggested that they all go to Poland to explore their roots. Dad was like iron. He refused even to discuss it. It was on his return from London that he had the massive heart attack and stroke that left him lying on that hospital bed like Jonah. I would like to go back and hold that unfamiliar hand in mine, still uncomfortably, but at least with some sense of the reality of this man lying on the white bed. I would like to talk to him about everything that I've discovered, and read him the book that I found which might help him to understand his own father. I wish that we could have made this journey together.

When Paul comes over, one evening, I drink tea, and watch him playing table tennis with the girls. I watch him laughing and teasing them over a dud shot. I am glad, after all that we have lived through, that we are here in this house together. It's just one moment among a thousand other moments. But this unexceptional moment is exactly what my father lost, the day he stepped on to the ship out of Poland. He did not know then that he would never share a moment of laughter, of anger, of love with Beniek again. He would have only silence.

After dinner, Paul and Wendy and I stand in the kitchen talking.

'How's the book going?' Paul asks, suddenly.

'Fine,' I say.

'I'd like to read it when it's finished,' he says. 'I guess you've found out quite a bit about the family? I always thought it would be a good thing to do, but I never really got around to it. When they came to visit me in London, I asked Dad if he wanted to go to Poland. And this look just came over his face.' I know exactly the look he is talking about.

'Fear,' I say.

Wendy is leaning against the bench. She looks at me.

'Fear?' she says.

'Yes,' I say. 'I think Dad was very afraid. And that is what I found the hardest thing to bear. I was scared of that fearful look in his eyes.'

'Yeah,' Paul says. He looks sad. Then, after a long while, he says, 'I remember the same look, once when I was a little kid, in Cafe Scheherezade in Acland Street. Dad was talking to two men in Yiddish. They were talking in low voices, with their heads bent close together. I couldn't understand what they were saying. Finally, Dad got up and told me we were going. He had that same look on his face. I knew not to ask him any questions. You're right. It was fear.'

'Yes,' I say. 'It's a shame. There were a lot of things I would have liked to ask.'

'I'm sorry I never asked him about it,' he says. 'But somehow, you just don't.'

'And there were things he could have learned, too.'

Paul nods.

'I think he was afraid,' I say. 'Afraid of what he might find, afraid of what it might do to him. And afraid for us, too.'

'Yes..

'It's strange. I guess he wasn't really a survivor of the Holocaust, because he wasn't there. But he lost more than most people ever do—almost everything he knew as a child, all his family, in one way or another ... But he was saved. I can't imagine how that must feel.'

'I have to go, now,' Paul says. 'I have someone waiting for me.'

Then, just before he goes, he turns and says.

'I really want to read that book.'

After Paul has left, Wendy and I start clearing up the dinner things.

'It's like the Pied Piper,' Wendy suddenly says.

'Sorry?' I say.

'I remember reading it to the girls when they were little. Do you know the story? He plays his pipe and leads all the children of the town into a cave, and the stone door closes behind them. But just one child is left behind, a lame child who couldn't follow. It's sad.'

I nod.

'Just what you were saying before,' she says. '*It* made me think of it.' She smiles at me, and goes on stacking the dishwasher.

What happens to the one who is left, I wonder. What happened to my father? For my mother, it was different. She was only a child, brought here by a mother and father to live among aunts and uncles and cousins. For my father there was nothing but a silence that only became thicker as the years passed. He was the lame child, sitting in silence, and hearing in his head the echoes of that strange, faraway music.

I think of the place where my father is buried. Tomorrow I will stand there for a long time. I will ask him about all of the things I want to know—about the sun shining on the nursery, the men in Cafe Scheherezade, the music flowing around the Saski Gardens, and the flapping of the leaves in the jungles of New Guinea. I will ask him why he stopped answering Ruth's letters, why he gave away the lighter I gave him as a present, and why he never spoke to me about any of these things. And I will remember Pinkus and Sara and Beniek and Gutka; Felicia and Nellie; my mother and her aunts and uncles and cousins on the pier; the line of soldiers walking along the dry riverbed; the shouts of the bookies; and even Reuben, who still goes in to his office every day. I will remember Warsaw, and New Guinea, and North Road and 18 Chapel Street, and the man in the jockey's costume riding the pantomime horse, and that voice, that familiar voice, my voice in the synagogue singing, *What do you see? I see a rod of an almond tree*.

Aaron's rod was made of almond wood. Although it was cut from the tree, it sprouted again, with new green shoots and small white blossoms.

After standing there for a long time, I will let the earth slip through my fingers on to his grave. Something will pass over, like a faint breath of wind disturbing the silence—my father's silence. It was a silence that he chose. It was also a silence that chose him.

But this is not my choice.

I have chosen to speak.

Bernard Marin AM was born in 1950 and graduated from the Prahran College of Advanced Education in Melbourne in 1970. He established his accounting practice in 1981 and currently works with the staff and partners of the practice as a consultant. Bernard has held a number of positions on various boards, including: Treasurer – Melbourne Writers Festival (2005–16), Koorie Heritage Trust (2000–08), and Liberty Victoria (de facto, 1984–92); board member – Australian Centre for Jewish Civilisation (2009–15), Reichstein Foundation (2011–12), Melbourne Community Foundation (2009–10), and Koorie Heritage Trust (2000–12).

Bernard is the author of Selection in Human Resource Accounting (1982); a memoir, My Father, My Father (Scribe, 2002), and Good as Gold: A Novel (Harvard Publications, 2017); *Stories of Profit and Loss* (Harvard Publications, 2019); *Stories of Remembering and Forgetting* (Harvard Publications, 2019) and *Letter to My Father* (Harvard Publications, 2019). Bernard lives in Melbourne with his wife, Wendy.

www.ingramcontent.com/pod-product-compliance
Lightning Source LLC
Chambersburg PA
CBHW020319010526
44107CB00054B/1907